FOREWORD

In editing the text, and checking the illustrations, I have been struck most by the wealth of information assembled in this series. For thirty years I have made a wide study of the animal kingdom, and while much of this information was already known to me, I was constantly coming upon an interesting fact or story which was entirely new to me. It is hoped therefore that readers of these volumes will be similarly entertained and informed.

Some of these stories struck me as so remarkable that I thought they must be untrue, yet, when I checked them, I found they were correct; or as correct as our knowledge takes us to the present day. For in dealing with animals you never know when knowledge that is accepted today may not be proven wrong tomorrow. One other thing that impressed me, as I searched the books and the libraries, or went to museums and zoos to check the details, or talked with scientists having special knowledge of particular animals, was that, in spite of the wealth of books on the subject, much of what is known about animals is inaccessible to all but the favoured few. The chief value of these books, therefore, is that so much information, otherwise scattered, and often difficult to obtain, has been brought together in a highly interesting form, and illustrated with vivid coloured drawings.

ANIMAL EXPLORERS AND WANDERERS

EDITED BY

MAURICE BURTON, D.Sc.

ODHAMS BOOKS LIMITED

LONG ACRE, LONDON

INTRODUCTION

This volume, ANIMAL EXPLORERS AND WANDERERS, tells the story of the migratory animals who travel amid the lonely outposts of the world. There are only a few thousand species, out of the million or more known, that undertake well-defined migrations but their populations are numbered by millions — vast flocks and herds — trooping in silent procession across the continents or the seas, following the cycle of the seasons across empty prairies, the boundless ocean or the limitless skies.

Some of these migratory wanderers, like the schools of whales and dolphins, have been known to man for thousands of years, yet much of their life beneath the ocean remains a mystery. Only now are we beginning to trace their journeys among the continents. Others, like the globe-trotting albatross, cover distances so vast that it staggers the imagination. Nothing seems to daunt the sea-going birds, not the limitless expanse of the ocean, nor the sudden storms that sweep the sky.

On land, the migrating herds of game animals still move across the vast Serengeti plains of Africa, breeding and pasturing as they travel from Lake Victoria to Mount Kilimanjaro, returning again to the lake before the rainy season. High above the plains, hidden in the cloud-capped forests, the rare mountain gorillas wander in small family groups among the bamboo brakes, marooned in their mountain refuge as surely as solitary seals on a sea-swept rock.

It is seldom that any two species migrate or wander in precisely the same way, nor do all those that are settled exploit their riches by the same means. In this volume we shall meet many of them for the first time: those that live like colonists, wresting a living in the waste places on the earth, and those that seem to wander like restless nomads about the sea and the sky. They are all part of a strange new world unfolded within the pages of this volume.

American red bat *(Lasiurus borealis)*

A MIGRATORY BAT

The **red bat** is found in southern Canada and the United States during the summer months. The most common of American bats, it sleeps during the day hanging among leaves, especially of oaks, and emerges at dusk to hunt for insects. At the first nip of autumn, however, the red bat forsakes this lonely way of life and, joining a small flock of its fellows, heads south towards Central America and the West Indies. These flocks, sometimes consisting solely of males or of females, fly on a steady course in contrast to the darting, swooping flight that they use when hunting insects. With its narrow tapering wings the red bat is, for its size, a flying machine of great speed and endurance. The mother bat bears two to four babies at a time, which she carries about for the first part of their life, their combined weight exceeding her own, a payload which must be the envy of every airline operator.

CREATURES OF BLIND DOOM

There are probably no more spectacular stories about animal migrations than those told about the five-inch **Norwegian lemming.** According to them vast numbers of lemmings come down from the mountains every few years, devouring the vegetation in their path, driven on by some blind force towards the sea, where they plunge in and are drowned. Only within the last few years has any real investigation been made into this, and the truth seems to be less spectacular than the traditional stories. The home of the lemmings is in the mountains where, every few years, their populations build up and the excess numbers spread outwards, bringing the lemmings down into the valleys, where they become something of a pest. Many are drowned in the rivers, some eventually reach the sea and are drowned. On the way, the snowy owl and other predators move in to take tremendous toll of them, and in due course this over-spill of lemmings is wiped out. In the next few years, the populations build up to another peak, there is again an exodus from the overcrowded habitat, and the story is repeated.

THE BIGGEST OF THEM ALL

If we could stand the biggest **blue whale** ever found on its tail, its snout would reach as high as the roof of a ten-storey building. This whale has been known to reach one hundred feet long and to weigh a hundred and twenty tons, which is about the same weight as twenty full-sized

Norwegian lemming (*Lemmus lemmus*)

elephants or seventeen hundred men. These dimensions make it the largest animal that has ever lived. During the southern summer the blue whales congregate in the Antarctic to feed on the abundant krill, a name given to the masses of shrimp-like animals swimming at the surface. For the southern winter they move towards the equator, into the warmer waters of the southern hemisphere, for the breeding season. There is little food here, and when summer comes again the blue whales, lean and ill-fed, move south again to fatten up on krill.

Blue whale (*Balaenoptera musculus*)

Finner whale or common rorqual *(Balaenoptera physalus)*

Sei whale *(Balaenoptera borealis)*

THE LARGE "GREYHOUND"

The **finner whale**, found in all the oceans of the world, is called the greyhound of the ocean because of its slender build and great speed in swimming. With an average length of seventy-five feet, and a maximum of eighty-two feet, it is indeed a large "greyhound" but one with extraordinary driving power and strength: and it can be bad-tempered, particularly – and understandably – when wounded by a harpoon. At such times a finner has been known to throw all its weight, force, and speed into blind fury, sometimes attacking the whaling ship from which the harpoon has been fired. In 1910 a woodenbarked whaler, the "Sorenson", was charged in this way by a finner travelling at twenty-five knots. The ship was ripped apart and sunk. A number of similar incidents have been recorded in the past sixty years. Another whale, firmly harpooned, towed a whaling ship with its engines going full speed astern at twelve knots before eventually – after a long thrashing fight – tiring itself out. These "greyhounds" are distributed over the seven seas but they are not common in polar seas. They may migrate from Greenland to Japan and from Chile to Alaska, and when on these long cruises they travel in large schools, travelling straight ahead and at a speed that taxes the whalers to overhaul them.

THAR SHE BLOWS

When the look-out high on the mountain sights the first **sei whale** spouting his white plume, the inhabitants of the Norwegian fiords know

that the whaling season has returned again. Every spring this whale makes its long journey from the warm waters of the equator, where it has spent the winter, to its summer feeding-grounds, the deep icy waters of the Arctic Ocean off the bleak Norwegian coast; the land of the Midnight Sun. This whale is called the Sei after the Seje or Coalfish, because it arrives in these Northern waters at the same time as this fish. In various parts of the world it undertakes seasonal migrations over long distances and, as with all migrations, these movements are linked with the supplies of food. That is, the whales move from one area to another as the seasonal supplies of small shrimp-like crustaceans, on which they feed, rise and fall in numbers.

It used to be thought that the whale's spout was due to the moisture in the warm breath condensing on contact with cold air, but since whales spout just as much in the Tropics as in the polar seas this cannot be the explanation. Now it is believed that the spout is formed of

Humpback whale (*Megaptera novaeangliae*)

droplets of mucus carried out from the lungs on the breath.

DEEPER THAN A SUBMARINE

How submarine-sailors, trapped and attacked with depth charges by an enemy destroyer, must wish their craft could dive as deep as a

Sperm whale (*Physeter catodon*)

Bottlenose whale *(Hyperoodon rostratus)*

whale! Although it had been long suspected, the whales' diving abilities were confirmed when a whale became entangled in a submarine cable and snapped it before becoming drowned at a depth of three thousand two hundred feet below the surface. This was discovered when the cable was brought to the surface for repairs. The great **humpback whale** is one that makes deep dives. With a short and deep body, the front of which is covered with knobs, it has very long flippers with which at times it will playfully smack a companion producing a noise that can be heard over a mile away. The humpback makes very regular migrations, to the cold seas to feed and to the warmer seas to breed. Because it tends to frequent the inshore waters, more is known than with most whales about the regular paths it follows in the seas.

THE WHALE WITH A TANK IN ITS HEAD

The **sperm whale,** the largest of the toothed whales, reaches a length of about sixty feet, and has a great tank-like head that contains a store of oil. This sperm oil was at one time used in lamps and for making candles. Also known as a cachalot, the sperm whale is the most famous of all the whales. It can submerge to the depth of over half a mile and stay below for up to an hour, then surface without any ill-effects. Its normal cruising speed is four knots per hour but it can treble this when necessary. This huge mammal feeds largely on squid, octopus and cuttlefish. Its long jaws and its numerous teeth enable it to seize and hold such slippery prey as giant squid. When fully grown it consumes something in the region of a ton of food a day, but is not fully

Blackfish or pilot whale *(Globicephala melaena)*

grown until its ninth year. Its lifespan is thought to be not much longer than twenty years. The sperm whale's head, which makes up one third of its entire length, is blunt or truncated in front and can be used as a huge battering ram, more than one old-time wooden whaling ship has had its side stove in like matchwood by it. The reservoir of liquid oil contained in the whale's head is thought to act as a protective cushion against excessive pressures when it descends to great depths. Today this oil, or spermaceti, is valued and used in the manufacture of soap and cosmetics. The most common large whale, and one found in all the oceans, the sperm whale can be identified by its spout, which is directed forward and upward in short puffs. When diving or sounding it raises its flukes high in the air and goes straight down. When at the surface it makes about sixty respirations every ten minutes. When nursing her young calf – which may measure fourteen-feet at birth and is born one year after mating – the mother sperm whale rolls over on her side, thus enabling the calf to breathe normally while feeding.

A VALUABLE PRIZE

Many a whaleboat owner has grown rich because of the huge schools of **bottlenose whales** that used to roam the North Atlantic. Their curious bulbous foreheads form receptacles for a very valuable fine wax similar to that obtained from sperm whales. In their quest for this natural wealth human hunters decimated the migrating herds of whales, some of which numbered hundreds of animals. The hunting, however, was not all one-sided. After the dreaded killer whale, the bottlenose is one of the most courageous and aggressive of whales. If one member of a school is wounded some of its comrades gather round to support it whilst another will charge the attacking boat, slashing it with its tail, ramming it or coming up underneath in an attempt to capsize it, until the terrified crew decide they have had enough and make off. The bottlenose changes colour as it grows older. From completely blue-black the male develops a cream-white head and the female becomes entirely light brown or yellow.

FOLLOW-MY-LEADER

Following their leader or pilot, large herds of the **blackfish** or **pilot whale** are found all over the Atlantic and Pacific oceans. The proverbial sheep are individualists compared with this whale. If the leader accidentally runs aground through venturing into shallow water all the herd follows. The Faroe Islanders have exploited this habit for centuries, watching for them as they follow their customary itinerary and driving the unfortunate animals into shallow channels where they can be massacred. The pilot whale grows to about thirty feet in length and is a different shape from all other whales. It has a short blunt head and a thick-necked

Sea bear (*Callorhinus ursinus*)

Chiru or Tibetan antelope *(Pantholops hodgsoni)*

to a hundred thousand at the beginning of this century, but, thanks to strict conservation laws, the world population of this sleek and elegant mammal is now back to its former size.

THE WARY ONE

The snow leopard stealthily inched forward with feline patience until with a roar it leaped at its prey – but to no avail. The **chiru,** its intended quarry, with split-second reflexes, bolted out of danger with the starting speed of a racing car. The Tibetan antelope, thirty-two inches at the shoulder and twenty-five pounds weight, is sociable, often travelling in groups of four or five, occasionally in large herds. Jackets and moccasins are made from its thick, close woolly fur. Nocturnal in habit, it lies up during the day in hollows in the sand, concealed until night descends. Yet even this stay-at-home must wander, and on the Tibetan plateau, which is its home, it will ascend to heights of 18,000 feet above sea-level, in quest of food on the bleak highlands.

WANDERERS OF THE NORTHLANDS

As spring comes to the Arctic and soft breezes melt the snow and expose the green of new growth on the northern treeless plains, the **caribou** begin to prepare for the annual

Caribou *(Rangifer arcticus)*

body that tapers towards its tail. Its dorsal fin is set far forward above its long thin flippers. The latest nuclear submarines are being built with hulls of a similar shape to this blunt-nosed body – a tribute to Nature as a naval architect! One of the toothed, as opposed to whalebone, whales, the pilot is nevertheless a warm-blooded mammal, and feeds its young with a milk not unlike rich cow's milk.

THE FUR SEAL

During most of the year the **sea bear** spends its time spread out over the Pacific Ocean, following the migrations of the squid and fish it feeds on. With the fast lengthening days of spring, however, it returns to the islands in the Bering Sea for the annual breeding fiesta. Here the sea bears assemble on the sun-baked rocks in their hundreds of thousands, the old males gathering large harems of females and guarding them jealously, the young males living in separate bachelor colonies. Sometimes known as the Alaska Fur Seal it provides the beautiful velvety pelts that can often be seen in furriers' windows. The wholesale slaughter of this seal for its fur resulted in its numbers being reduced

13

Caribou *(Rangifer arcticus)*

summer migration northward. They have spent the winter on the edge of the forest and by age-old custom they travel hundreds of miles to the summer feeding grounds on the Arctic tundra. Each year they follow the same routes - despite many waiting dangers and hardships. Day by day these antlered wanderers gather together as if assembling on parade. Then, in straggling formation, with cows and yearlings leading and the bulls lagging several days behind, they begin their march northward across the greening tundra, swimming rivers and lakes. The cows stop at last to have their calves. In about two weeks when the new calves have strength to travel and as autumn is approaching, the herd starts out again on their long slow journey back to the forests of the south. Now the males lead. Their normally thick woolly coats are thin and shabby for this is the moulting time. Swarms of flies lay their eggs in the caribou's hide and make

life almost unbearable. Consequently, the herds walk slowly and so become an easy prey to wolves and hunters.

CANADA'S GOOSE

In October, the **Canada goose** leaves the marshes and lakes in the far north of Canada's Hudson Bay region and wanders south to North Carolina and Florida. Flying in V-formation, it migrates in very large flocks. When these birds wish to rest in mid-air, they stop flapping their wings and glide. Arriving in the southern marshlands, these migrants are very hungry and must immediately begin the task of finding food. Some of them seize underwater shellfish and crabs, whilst others feed upon the tender roots and shoots of water plants. Each year the geese follow much the same routes on migration, but the more interesting feature concerns their return flight in spring. Many other migrating birds speed up their flight as the waves of migrants approach their breeding grounds. By contrast, the movement north of the Canada geese to their breeding grounds is a steady, uniform progression, and it has been found to correspond with the movement of the isotherm of 35º F, so that they enjoy the same temperature all the way.

SNOW STORM OF GEESE

The bleak, isolated marshy tundra of northern Canada is the breeding ground for the pure-white **snow goose.** In this bitterly cold land, the female chooses a grassy spot to lay her ten eggs. One day after they hatch, the down-covered babies take to the icy water. Aerial photographs have revealed that within a relatively small area, as many as forty thousand of these birds can congregate. This is almost the entire population of the species. Hunters have left this breeding ground undisturbed, only because it is so isolated that few men can ever enter. This great group of young geese and their parents forage together for the roots of water plants; if they do not find enough of them, they turn to the vegetation and graze like cattle. When the young are old enough to fly, the whole colony of geese, looking like a gigantic snowstorm, takes to the air. After travelling south together a certain distance, they split up; some go south-east to the Atlantic Ocean; others go south-west to California.

ROUGH-WATER DUCK

An excellent swimmer and diver, the eighteen-inch **harlequin duck** uses the land mainly for nesting. After a silent courtship, since neither the male nor the female uses the voice much, a nest is made amid grass, under bushes or in a hollow tree stump, never far from the water's edge. While the female incubates the eggs, the male remains on guard in the water, and as soon as the young hatch they leave the nest for the water and soon become used to rough water. The birds forage in the rapids of streams or in the surf on the coast, feeding on aquatic animals such as fish, frogs, small crustaceans and molluscs, most of it obtained by diving. Their summer breeding grounds extend from the Aleutian Islands and Alaska across to Labrador and Greenland. In autumn they do not go far south, and they keep to the coasts often feeding among ice floes, and return north again before winter is past.

FISH FLAVOURED DUCK

The water-fowl known as the **velvet scoter** spends much of the year near the tree-line between the tundra and the pine forests of Europe and Asia. It is seldom hunted, not because it lives in such isolated places but because its flesh has a poor flavour. Its food is mainly marine molluscs, although it takes some crustaceans, a few fish and some vegetable matter,

1. **Canada goose** (*Branta canadensis*)
2. **Velvet scoter** (*Melanitta fusca*)
3. **Snow goose** (*Anser caerulescens*)
4. **Harlequin duck** (*Histrionicus histrionicus*)

and much of this is obtained by diving. The velvet scoter may stay under water for as much as two minutes, diving to as much as 66 feet. In early summer these ducks nest on rocky islets in the Baltic or high up in the Arctic in deep crevices in peat, the newly-hatched ducklings going straight to water. In autumn, they move south, mainly to the Baltic and North Sea, but some reach as far as Spain and the Black Sea.

HIGH-FLYING MIGRANTS

On the shores of deep lakes high in the mountains of Tibet lives the grey and white **bar-headed goose** that flies south each October to winter on the rivers which twist through Burma, northern India, and Pakistan. There it stays until mid-March, resting in flocks by day on dry sandbanks in the middle of favoured rivers. When twilight approaches, the bar-headed geese take to the air, flying in V-formation or in long, straight lines, to where they can feed on shoots in fields of peas, beans and grain. After feeding all night, they return at dawn to their river resting-places. When March is half over, the thirty-inch long bar-headed geese – named for the two dark bands across the back of the head – return north to nest among the lush grasses which border their native lakes, their nests being lined with their own warm down and feathers. Three to four ivory-coloured eggs are laid and the goslings hatching from these are strong enough by

October to accompany their parents on their long and very high flight south. These birds need to fly high to cross the Himalayas, and one skein of bar-headed geese is estimated to have flown from 5,000 to 15,000 feet. They are helped in this by having a larger area of wing in relation to the body than other geese.

SQUADRONS IN THE SKY

With a lumbering take-off, running on water, pounding the surface with its webbed feet and often striking it with its wing tips, the world's largest living goose finally clears its watery runway. High in the sky in perfect V-formation, its deep honking resounding afar, the **swan goose's** noisy flight to its summer home in the marshy, rolling tundra of northern East Asia is extremely powerful and much swifter than it appears. The leading bird in the V changes from time to time as the birds soar on at speeds of up to fifty miles an hour for sometimes as much as two thousand miles. How does it steer this course as it flies a mile or two above the land and sea? Some of it is done by landmarks, but not when the birds travel mostly at night. It used to be supposed that birds are guided by the earth's magnetism or that they can feel the rotation of the earth in their ears just as we can feel the rotation of a merry-go-round. The truth seems to be that birds are guided by the length of day in timing the start of their migrations, and that they navigate by the skies, using the sun by day and the stars by night. One thing

Bar-headed goose (*Anser indicus*)

almost anything vegetable or animal. Shelduck are distributed over Europe and Asia and they are, for the most part, resident and non-migratory. They have, however, one peculiarity which they share with some other ducks, that they migrate to moult. The shelduck of the British Isles, for example, migrate in large flocks in July to the area around Heligoland. There all their flight feathers drop off at once, so that the birds are unable to fly. Having completed the moult they return in slow stages to their breeding grounds. From the time that

Swan goose
(Anser cygnoides)

is certain, a migrating bird released on a clear night will fly unerringly on its course but will tend to be lost if the sky becomes overcast.

MIGRATING TO MOULT

Male and female **shelduck** are alike, the two being distinguishable only in the breeding season, when the male develops a large knob on the beak. They favour the sandy dunes for nesting, the nest being situated in dark places, especially in holes in trees and in old burrows, but they feed especially in the muddy estuaries, chiefly on molluscs, although they will take

Shelduck (*Tadorna tadorna*)

the flight feathers drop out until they have grown again the plumage of both sexes is much the same, although the female is a little duller than the male, and she lacks the knob at the base of the bill.

Mallard (*Anas platyrhynchos*)

NO ORDINARY FLIER

The **mallard** is the most widely distributed of the world's ducks, being found throughout Europe, most of Asia and North America. In winter it may be seen in North Africa, even as far south as Borneo, in Asia, and Panama and the West Indies, in the New World. Nevertheless, the mallard is only partially migratory, large numbers of the total population spending the whole year in the same area. This is not due to any inability to make long journeys for mallard are strong fliers and on migration have been recorded in the United States as travelling at 45 to 60 miles per hour. When they do migrate there is nothing random about their journeys. In North America, for example, they use the same flyway as the Canada geese, which takes them over the main river basins, including the Mississippi Valley, to wintering grounds on the shores of the Gulf of Mexico. As might be expected, with so common a bird, more attention has been paid to their movements than to those of other ducks, and two interesting facts have emerged. For example, the experiment was tried of taking eggs from Britain and hatching them in Finland. The ducks hatching from these migrated with the Finnish mallard – which is, perhaps, what one

White stork *(Ciconia ciconia)*

Black stork *(Ciconia nigra)*

would have expected! Another observation, although this applies to a few other species of ducks as well, is that individual mallard will sometimes fly north in spring, to a new summer ground, without having made a corresponding journey south the previous year. Such birds are spoken of as abmigrants.

THE VANISHING STORK

After a few trial jumps, the **white stork** takes to the air, to join the flock migrating from South Africa to Europe where in March and April the pairs return often to the same town, the same house, even to the same roof top as the year before. People encourage them by placing on the chimney stack a wicker basket as a ready-made nest. Three to five white eggs are laid, the parents sharing the incubation, which lasts just over a month. To feed the young and themselves, the white storks search the fields and swamps for small animals, including insects, freshwater shrimps, frogs, eels, mice, moles, even small birds. Although in the Western world the stork is traditionally a bringer of human babies, it has difficulty in ensuring the survival of its own young, for as a race storks seem to be vanishing. They no longer nest in Switzerland and in many parts of France, and in Holland and Germany their numbers have seriously declined. This may be due to their migrations, for flocks wintering in South Africa spend the season hunting locusts, and it is suspected that the heavy use of insec-

ticides against these insect plagues may have greatly reduced the storks' food-supply. The white storks migrate along two routes: through Spain to Africa across the Straits of Gibraltar; and through Asia Minor to Egypt, thence along the Nile valley to southern Africa.

The **black stork** is thirty-eight inches high, only slightly smaller than its white cousin. Its range and migration pattern are similar, save that its numbers are greater in Asia. This is unfortunate for its survival, for unlike the white stork it is not held as a symbol of good luck by Europeans. Little help is given it in building a nest, so it constructs it on some rocky cliff or in the fork of a tree. The male brings the twigs and grasses for the female, who does most of the work of shaping the nest. The reason why the storks take these two migration routes, and it is also why there are no storks in the British Isles, is that no stork will cross a sheet of water unless it can see the opposite shore. Another interesting feature of stork migration is that even without the knowledge gained from ringing them, much was learned from the arrowheads some of them carried, which struck them without killing. The shapes of the arrow-heads showed from which district in Africa the storks had journeyed.

THE RUNNING BIRD

In the temperate zones of Europe, Asia and Africa, wherever the vegetation is not too dense, the **common quail** may be found. An unpretentious-looking bird only ten inches long, with brown and white markings, it is one of the most sought after of game-birds and leads a life fraught with peril. At one time it used to migrate in great hordes from Europe and western Asia into North Africa, the only member of the pheasant family that is migratory. Now its numbers have been so reduced that is is most often seen alone or in small coveys. Although it seems to rise into the air with difficulty, it can fly well, and travels at speeds of up to 57 miles per hour on migration. Its usual habit is, however, especially, when being hunted, to scurry over the ground, hidden in the grass, rather than expose itself in the air. The quail can even swim if it has to, but, by and large, it is one of the most land-loving of all birds, which makes its long migrations the more remarkable. Years ago, quail migrated in phenomenal numbers, but during the last century they were killed by the million for market.

A CROWNED BIRD

A trumpet call from high up in the sky announces the coming of one of the world's most striking birds, the **crowned crane.** On its head it wears a gorgeous crown of golden bristles. The eyes are wonderfully clear, like jewels; and the colour contrast of grey neck, snow-white cheeks and pitch-black head is pleasing indeed. For feeding, this bird walks

Common quail *(Coturnix coturnix)*

about the marsh-lands, stamping its feet to drive up insects which it can then seize. The crowned crane is quite widely distributed. It is found in flocks along the Nile; along the coasts of the great lakes of the Congo and East Africa; in the humid rain forests; even as far south as the tip of Africa, the Cape of Good Hope. These three-foot tall creatures are usually described as resident. If taken literally, this would mean that

African crowned crane *(Balearica pavonina)*

each stays in the same place all the year round. Yet even the crowned cranes move about from one place to another as the seasons pass, moving from one feeding ground to another.

THE SPECIALISTS

To illustrate how varied are the migrations in different species of birds we can consider this random collection of wading birds. The **limpkin,** of America, is a good example of a completely non-migratory bird. It lives in the marshes and damp forests, from South Carolina in the United States to the Argentine. It lives mainly on molluscs and is expert at extracting the soft body from the shell, but it also takes other small animals found in marshes. Not only is there little need for limpkins to migrate, because they have abundant food all around, they are also poor flyers. They do not fly often, and when they do they take a short run and then fly weakly with the wings held high over their backs. The **European snipe** is sedentary in some parts of its range and migratory in other parts. Even the sedentary populations move perhaps twenty to thirty miles from winter to summer, and the migratory birds pass to Africa in late summer, returning to Europe in spring. One feature of the snipe's migrations is that they are dependent on the weather, in contrast to so many of the better-known migrants, such as swifts, which arrive on their summer breeding grounds almost to the day each year. The **woodcock,** another European bird, also migrates with the weather, and close study of these birds in Hungary has shown that they arrive there from Africa any time between the beginning of March and early April. Moreover, comparison of this with weather charts has shown that its arrival in Hungary always coincides with a depression over western Europe, especially over the British Isles. The **curlew** is another "weather bird". The migrating flocks are always larger on stormy days and they begin to take off on their migratory flights several hours before the onset of a storm. Thus their arrival in a district heralds the approach of a storm, when the flocks are large. Weather affects the **black-winged stilt** in a different way. Their populations are sometimes non-migratory, sometimes migratory, but their movements are always erratic. They feed in the margins of shallow ponds or on mud-flats, which may dry

1. **Limpkin** (*Aramus guarauna*)
2. **European snipe** (*Gallinago gallinago*)
3. **European woodcock** (*Scolopax rusticola*)
4. **Curlew** (*Numenius arquata*)
5. **Black-winged stilt** (*Himantopus himantopus*)
6. **European avocet** (*Recurvirostra avosetta*)
7. **American avocet** (*Recurvirostra americana*)

up in a period of drought, or be extensive in a continued wet spell, and this instability of the habitat has its effect on the movements of the stilt. The **American avocet** has only a limited annual migration: in summer to roughly the northern half of the United States, and over the border into Canada; in winter to the southern United States, Mexico and Central America. But there are a number of occasions when it has been reported much farther afield, from Cuba and Jamaica, and from Greenland. The summer migration of the least sandpiper may take it as far north as Alaska, its winter migration as far south as Brazil. Some individuals are great wanderers, however, occasionally reaching Europe and Asia.

WINGS RESERVED FOR MIGRATION

Although the loud, harsh voice of the **water rail** is often heard near ponds, lakes and marshlands, in Europe and parts of temperate Asia, the bird is seldom seen, for it keeps to thick reed beds and other waterside cover. When it does expose itself it is always ready to dash back into cover by diving underwater to reach it. So it is difficult to flush because it seldom takes to the air and it can tread reeds faster than its pursuers, its long toes enabling it to move easily over soft vegetation or mud. When it comes to migrating, however, the water rail flies strongly and over enormous distances. The wintering grounds cover the whole of Africa and southern Asia. The birds fly by night and on the northward journey in spring may sometimes overshoot the mark. The water rail breeds in Iceland but sometimes individuals go beyond this and touch down in Greenland. The water rail has even turned up in the West Indies, thousands of miles off its regular beat.

On the previous page we dealt with seven birds living in wet places. They all have two other things in common: long legs and a long bill. The water rail has these as well, and it also frequents wet places. Yet the seven belong to a different order from that in which the rails are placed. This emphasizes that we cannot always be sure from the appearance of a bird where it belongs in the classification. This is because the classification is to a large extent based on the internal anatomy. The seven birds shown on page twenty-one belong to a group which used to be called the waders, and it has been said that any field observer of ordinary experience will recognize a wader when he sees

one, even if it belongs to a species he has not known before. Since we are about to deal with more waders it may be useful to say what are the signs by which the field observer picks them out from other kinds of birds. Quite clearly, when we compare these with the water rail we see that it is not sufficient merely to say that waders have long legs and a long slender bill. Indeed, if we compare the rail with the turnstone and the pratincole, shown in the picture at the bottom of the next page, we see at once

Water rail (*Rallus aquaticus*)

that something more is needed.

Although a few waders, such as woodcock and snipe, keep very much to the woodlands, most waders live in the open country and make no attempt to hide among vegetation. They have little need to do so because they have a sufficient camouflage in their plumage. Some are found on marshes well inland, some are more often seen on the shore or on salt marshes around estuaries, while others may be met in either of these habitats. It is when they take to the wing that most of the waders reveal themselves. They fly rapidly, with a quick wing action. In most of them the wings are pointed rather than rounded. As they fly their legs trail backwards, under the tail. Above all, most waders do not extend the wings fully when flying, so that the wings appear angled. Many waders, also, tend to fly on a zig-zag course, or to bank and swerve as they go. Another feature is that typically waders call as they fly, and they have a more or less mournful whistle, as mournful as the misty marshes in which so many of them live. There are exceptions, as might be expected. The lapwing, for example, has rounded wings and a slow flapping flight, but it has the mournful call, after which it receives its second name, peewit. Waders migrate at night and then we can hear their plaintive calls although the birds themselves are invisible.

THE LOCUST BIRD

When not hawking insects on the wing, the **swallow plover** or **pratincole** runs them down on the ground so efficiently that it is known as the "Locust Bird" in South Africa. Although its bill is small it can be opened very wide, and few insects are fast or agile enough to evade this airborne pursuit. When not feeding, this dainty bird, with the smooth clean lines and forked tail of a born aerial acrobat, struts and bobs about, stretching up from time to time on tiptoe for a look around. And any insect it sees has as much chance of escape as an old propeller-driven biplane with a modern jet on its tail. The pratincole is African but part of its population migrates into southern Europe and south-west Asia for the summer.

A SPECIALIST AT KILLING

Among the countless animals exposed each day by the ebbing tide are limpets, clams and mussels. In the first few minutes after they are exposed the shells of bivalves remain open as when under water. The **oystercatcher** can then thrust its long bill deep into the soft flesh inside, severing and paralyzing the muscles that would close the hard protective shells. The

bird is also adept at knocking limpets from their firm hold on rocks. Oystercatchers are found discontinuously over most of the world, along the coasts. They are absent from much of southern and south-eastern Asia, for example, and from Africa except for the south-west tip. They inhabit, however, a large inland area of central Asia. Everywhere they are predominantly sedentary, but in the most southerly as well as the most northerly parts of their range there are irregular migratory movements. Those in the north seem to be in the nature of mass flights to escape the worst effects of freezing temperatures.

A CURIOUS FEEDER

The **turnstone** spends most of its time turning over with its beak the stones and debris that litter the beach, for the small animal life gathered underneath. This winged beachcomber, vividly marked with dark browns, blacks and white, with deep orange legs, spends the summer breeding season amid the islands and coasts bordering the Arctic Ocean, as well as those in the Baltic and the Bering Straits. Outside the breeding season the turnstone is one of the greatest migrants among birds. It is then found, solitary or in small flocks in such distant places as Chile, South Africa, Australia, and New Zealand, and the islands of Polynesia.

1. **Pratincole or swallow plover** *(Glareola pratincola)*
2. **Oystercatcher** *(Haematopus ostralegus)*

3. **Ruddy turnstone** *(Arenaria interpres)*

Rufous hummingbird *(Selasphorus rufus)*

THE WORLD TRAVELLER

An unpretentious-looking bird called the **American golden plover,** ten inches long with black and brownish colouring and golden spots, makes one of the longest treks of any living creature, and one of the most extraordinary. When in flocks the golden plovers make a strange rattling sound as they swoop and dive in unison. On the ground, they lose their grace and when hunting insects look like mechanical birds. They run in short spurts, halt abruptly and freeze. Then they jerk down to pick up a tempting insect, and dart off to repeat the process somewhere else. After nesting in Alaska and northern Canada huge flocks gather in Labrador and journey in an arc, over the ocean, to the coast of Brazil, a distance of 2,400 miles. On the return north the following spring, however, they cross South America to Central America and then fly north by way of the Mississippi Valley to their Arctic breeding grounds. But, strangely, the young birds fly overland all the way in both directions. There is another species of golden plover *(Pluvialis apricaria)* which ranges widely across Europe and Asia.

American golden plover *(Pluvialis dominica)*

AN EXTRA FUEL TANK

Summer in Alaska, winter in Mexico; this is not a description of a millionaire's way of life but of the manner in which the **rufous hummingbird** spends its year. Each autumn it heads south, travelling at least two thousand miles to its winter quarters. How such tiny birds can perform a tremendous feat of endurance like this is something of a mystery, but the hummingbirds manage it without too many dropping out on the way. One thing we do know is that in order to provide a source of energy during its migratory flight, the rufous hummingbird puts on extra fat. Some hummingbirds add as much as fifty percent to their normal weight. This load, all fat, is like an extra fuel tank for their flight. It could be compared to a twelve-stone man putting on six stone of fat in preparation for a short period of exertion during which he could neither eat nor sleep. Hummingbirds, also, can conserve energy. One way they do this is to go into a sort of hibernation when they sleep. The temperature of most birds drops a little at night, but in hummingbirds it drops almost to that of the surrounding air.

TWO NUMBER-TWO SWIFTIES

Among the fastest flying birds are the swifts, whose speed is topped only by their close relative, the hummingbird, and exceeded only by the hawks and falcons. But for sustained flight no bird matches the swift, that spends most of its time cutting through the air with its long sickle-shaped wings at a pace which gives it its name. There are one hundred and fifty different kinds of swifts, and two of the more interesting are the **brown-throated spinetail swift** of south-east Asia, and its American cousin, the **chimney swift**. The sombre-plumaged Asian species, a common bird in Indo-China and Malaya, wheels through the skies in big, scattered flocks. Perhaps for a month or so, the flocks settle in one district, then move to another area that takes their fancy. The sooty black, sparrow-sized **chimney swift** of the eastern and western United States

Common swift (*Apus apus*)

Brown-throated spinetail swift
(*Chaetura gigantea*)
Chimney swift
(*Chaetura pelagica*)

MIGRATIONS TO AVOID STORMS

The **common swift** spends long hours in the air swooping, gliding, and flying at high speed in pursuit of flying insects. Against grey skies these dark-coloured birds seem to show up more and in strong winds they appear to be in their element. As night falls the females return to the nests, to their eggs or their young, but the males, it seems, fly to a great height to roost in the skies, floating on the currents of air until morning. Swifts spend most of the year in South Africa and come north, to Europe and Asia, for a fairly short breeding season. This means a very long journey for a bird seven inches long and weighing just over an ounce. But more remarkable are their migrations to avoid storms. Long before an electric storm reaches the area they are in the swifts fly anything up to 800 miles out of the path of the storm. Meanwhile, their nestlings go into a state resembling hibernation, until the parents return to start feeding them once more.

is aptly named, because it builds its saucer-shaped nest inside chimneys, gluing twigs together with its own sticky saliva. Each autumn, the chimney swift leaves its native United States and flies on rapid wingbeats to warm, far-away Peru, in South America, returning in spring.

DERBY AND JOAN

The bright and brilliant **golden oriole** winters in East Africa. A starling-sized bird with twelve tail feathers, it has a raucous cat-like cry, but its song is flute-like. The female is green; and the nest built by the pair of them is cup-shaped and woven of bark fibres and grass. Both birds share the task of incubation, and both feed the young. The golden oriole makes what is called a migration loop, and another peculiarity is that its migration route is always along a north-west and south-east line. Thus, from East Africa it flies to Europe via Libya, Tunisia and Italy and makes the return journey across Greece, the Aegean Sea and Egypt.

European golden oriole
(Oriolus oriolus)

STARLINGS FLY IN ALL DIRECTIONS

Starlings are common over most of Europe and western Asia. Their formation-flying is a wonderful spectacle, as they wheel and swoop, and turn as if receiving orders from a leader. In contrast with the elegant precision of its flying the starling's nest is untidy, a scruffy mixture of straw, leaves, twigs, feathers, in fact anything the bird can manage to scrounge. The nest may be in a hollow in a tree, in the

roof-space, or in an old wall, and starlings are much given to taking over garden nesting boxes. We are apt to think of starlings as non-migratory because they are with us all the year. In fact, they demonstrate every phase of sedentary, nomadic and migratory conditions. There is the movement of young starlings, for example, which scatter almost as soon as they can fly, travelling in due course as much as three hundred miles from their starting-point. Then we have the situation in which adult starlings migrate in autumn from North Ger-

Common (European) starling *(Sturnus vulgaris)*

many to Britain while those from Scandinavia fly south through Belgium to France, and those from southern Germany go to Spain, Italy and North Africa.

THE SINGING BERRY-EATER

The **mistle thrush** is noted for its predilection for eating mistletoe berries. It is even more renowned for the circumstances under which it sings. As the winter draws to a close in Europe one of the most noticeable songs is that of the mistle thrush, but not because it is then particularly beautiful. It is a welcome sound, because it heralds the approach of spring, but it soon becomes drowned in the spring chorus of other songsters. The time when a mistle thrush is heard at its best is in dirty weather. We see it perched at the top of a sapling when the wind is blowing so hard that the young tree rocks backwards and forwards, carrying the mistle thrush with it. Yet the bird continues to sing with all its might. At other times we can hear the mistle thrush singing during a snowstorm. These are reasons why, in Britain, the bird is called the Stormcock. We would expect such a bird not to migrate south in winter, and, in fact, it is sedentary except in the most northerly parts of its range. There the mistle thrushes do move south for the winter – but not very far south.

Mistle thrush
(Turdus viscivorus)

THE WANDERING TROUBADOUR

In spring and summer this wonderful songster, the handsome black, white and buff-coloured **bobolink** nests among tall grasses in meadows of Canada and northern and central United States, filling the air with his tinkling melody, which makes him the best singing bird in all North America. When the last days of autumn tell the coming of winter, the seven-inch bobolink and his drab-hued mate, in company with others of their kind, make a very long migration, all the way to northern Argentina, a distance of about seven thousand miles. On the way, they settle briefly on the islands of Cuba and Jamaica, then continue to South America, a feat attempted by few migrating North American birds, who usually shun long flights over water. Over hundreds of miles of Amazon forests and endless grasslands, the dauntless bobolinks push on. At last, after weeks of flying, they arrive in the heart of South America, where they spend the winter, returning to their North American homes in early spring. Wherever they may have been

during the summer they all make for the eastern United States, and this route, down through Florida and across to South America is known as the Bobolink Route.

Bobolink *(Dolichonyx oryzivorus)*

Migration route of the bobolink

28

STAY-AT-HOME PLOVERS

The black-crested bird, twelve inches long, with the iridescent green and bronze plumage, is known as the **lapwing.** It nests on marshes and moorlands, and is commonly seen on cultivated land, the nest being no more than a scrape in the earth to contain the four brown eggs heavily marked with black. Most of the lapwings are sedentary, remaining in one area throughout the year. There is a slight movement towards southern Europe, and some individuals even cross to North Africa for the winter, but there is no clear-cut migratory movement. There is to begin with what is called a post-juvenile dispersal, when young birds merely scatter in all directions. Then, in autumn all lapwings do one of three things: they either stay where they are, or move south-west or move west. But none moves very far.

HENPECKED

In autumn, **Wilson's phalarope** leaves its

Lapwing or green plover *(Vanellus vanellus)*

summer homeland, the inland lakes of North America, and migrates south to the Pacific coast of Chile and to the pampas of Argentina. Not only is this bird gifted with good powers of flight, it can wade, walk and swim with equal skill, and a favourite trick is to wade into shallow water and whirl around in small circles like a top, flushing small animals from the mud. The female Wilson's phalarope is larger than the male, and she does the wooing. Moreover, after mating she selects the nesting site and the "henpecked" husband builds the nest. When she has laid her eggs she flies away, leaving her mate to incubate the eggs, and care for the young. Towards the end of summer, the females gather into flocks, and when the time comes to migrate south the males join them.

In most birds either the cock and the hen are coloured much the same or the cock is more brightly coloured than the hen. Where the two have a similar plumage, we find that both sexes usually share the nest-building, the incub-

Wilson's phalarope *(Steganopus tricolor)*

ation of the eggs and the care of the young birds. In those species in which the cock is more brightly coloured than the hen, she it is that does most if not all the nest-building and the incubation. The cock may help but only to a slight extent. There is no rule in this, but the tendency is for the responsibilities to be partitioned in this way. Species in which the hen is more brightly coloured than the cock are few. Where we find this, however, it usually happens that the cock takes over all the parental duties except the actual laying of the eggs. It is better for the parent that is less brightly coloured to incubate since this makes the nest less conspicuous.

WHERE MIGRATION IS A DANGER

Four thousand years before the birth of Christ, a man drew on the walls of a cave at Tajo Segura, in southern Spain, a crude picture of a long-legged, stork-like bird which he had seen flying through the autumn sky. Today, the descendants of this bird, the **European spoonbill,** occupy breeding grounds stretching from western Europe eastward to India, and southwards into North Africa. This sociable, three-foot long bird nests in wet marshes and feeds by wading in shallow water on its long black legs, swinging its eight-inch long, spoon-like

1. **European spoonbill**
   (*Platalea leucorodia*)
2. **Roseate spoonbill**
   (*Ajaia ajaja*)

beak from side to side in the water, scooping up seeds and small animals. There is little migratory movement and even this is more a matter of spoonbills in the northern part of the range moving slightly south. It is quite different for the **roseate spoonbill** of America, seen in the left-hand corner of our picture. This formerly existed in large numbers but was persecuted until only a small remnant remained in Florida. This has been given protection by law, but the trouble is that this species is migratory, and in those parts of South America where it goes for the winter there is less concern about protecting this rare species.

A LONE WANDERER

In the quiet of a summer evening as the ears of wheat wave gently in the breeze, a strange "churring" sound tells us the **common nightjar** is preparing for its nightly pursuit of insects on the wing. The bird rests on the ground by day, marvellously hidden by its mottled brown and grey plumage. In June the female lays two marbled eggs direct on the ground, making no attempt to build a nest,

and these are even more difficult to find. After several weeks the eggs hatch, the young nightjars grow rapidly and by the end of the summer they and their parents make the long migration back to Africa. The extraordinary part of this story is that there are well over a dozen species in Africa, but only this one species makes the long journey north to breed.

Common nightjar (*Caprimulgus europaeus*)

THE WORLD'S LONG-DISTANCE FLIER

The most striking migration of all is that made by the fifteen-inch long **arctic tern,** which each year flies over twenty-two thousand miles, from the Arctic to the Antarctic and back, a journey equal to the entire distance around the earth! During the Arctic spring and summer, it breeds in colonies north of the Arctic Circle. Beginning in July and reaching a peak in September, the terns of arctic America fly east to join those of arctic Europe. Then all fly down the eastern Atlantic to spend the southern spring and summer in the Antarctic. In this way, they see more daylight than any other animal, because for eight months of the year they have twenty-four hours of daylight each day and for the other four months they have more daylight than darkness. They travel singly or in groups of up to twenty-five, never in a straight line of route but flying erratically.

Arriving in the Antarctic, they meet other arctic terns who have bred in north-east Siberia and Alaska, and who have flown down the eastern Pacific parallel with the western coasts of North and South America. After spending the southern summer in the Antarctic, many living during this time among the pack-ice, the terns fly back to the Arctic by the same route, flying over the sea the whole time. Some arctic terns fly all the way down the Atlantic to fetch up on one tiny oceanic island.

THE SEA-SKIMMING TRAVELLER

Another of the world's great travellers is the sea-skimming, brown and white **great shearwater.** In rock crevices on the tiny, isolated islands of Tristan da Cunha in the middle of the Atlantic Ocean, well south of the equator, this bird breeds in vast numbers. When the cold weather comes to this lonely part of the world,

Arctic tern (*Sterna paradisaea*)

31

Great shearwater
(Puffinus gravis)

THEY DIE FOR LIFE

Hundreds of millions of **salmon** are caught and canned yearly. They range from the enormous Chinook, of 90 lbs. or more, to the Humpback of three to five lbs., which fills most of the cans. But what of the fish itself? How does it continue to survive? The answer is one of Nature's miracles. Eggs are laid in vast numbers near the headwaters of many North American rivers, after which the parent fish die. Weeks later the eggs hatch and a new generation swarms into life. After about a year the young salmon go down to the sea in untold millions. They stay in the deeps for three to seven years, feeding mainly on herring or other small fish. Then, full of strength, the mating urge comes upon them, and by some instinct which is not yet fully understood they return to the exact place of their birth! Finding the river mouth, they battle upstream, leap over rocks and rapids, rarely feeding, and reach their goal with just enough strength to spawn. Then, in turn, they die – after having created yet another generation.

it flies thousands of miles north, following the prevailing winds, to pass spring and summer in the North Atlantic. Far out at sea the great shearwater stays, only exceptionally coming to land when driven there by a storm. Watching it flying just above the waves, tilting its eighteen-inch body first one way, then the other, it is easy to see how this graceful seabird acquired its name. Gliding on almost motionless wings, it swoops down into the hollows of enormous waves to pick fish and squid from the sea with its hooked beak. In June, huge flocks of great shearwaters can for days be seen hovering over the great Newfoundland fishing grounds, scavenging pieces of fish offal from the sea after the hardy North Atlantic fishermen have cleaned their catch. In August they move into the eastern North Atlantic, and in the autumn they begin their flight south to Tristan da Cunha, where in 1961 the British government evacuated the inhabitants because of dangerous volcanoes. But two years later, most of the homesick men and women returned to their beloved lonely islands – just as the world's four or five million great shearwaters return each year from their far-away North Atlantic fishing grounds.

Salmon *(Salmonidae)*

European eel (*Anguilla anguilla*)

American eel (*Anguilla rostrata*)

THE MYSTERY OF EEL MIGRATION

Following an instinct, upon the origin and nature of which we can only speculate, the five-feet long, twelve-year-old female **European eels** leave their home in the rivers and lakes of Europe, plunge into the Atlantic Ocean, and in company with twenty-inch males, journey across three thousand miles of the Atlantic Ocean, each to lay one million eggs in the Sargasso Sea, near Bermuda. This amazing trip begins in autumn and takes an entire year, and the eels eat nothing on their long journey. When they arrive, having changed colour during the trip from yellow to silver, they swim down fifteen hundred feet to a warm and highly salty layer of water. There the females lay their eggs and die. The males shed their milt and also die. From the fertilised eggs hatch larval eels, one of which is shown at the top in the accompanying picture. It resembles a willow leaf, except that it is transparent, and it is called a leptocephalus. The leptocephali then instinctively start the long return voyage to Europe, aided by the currents of the warm Gulf Stream, as drawn on the accompanying map, a journey which takes almost three years. During the trip, the leptocephalus grows to about three inches long and when it reaches the coasts of Europe it changes into a small eel, known as an elver, which is seen at the bottom of the picture. Each spring, millions of elvers enter the rivers and make their way upstream to the fresh-water habitats from which their dead parents came. During this migration up the rivers large quantities of elvers are caught and eaten as a delicacy. The **American eels** also leave their native fresh waters to spawn

Stages in a young eel's development

Map showing the journeys of eels

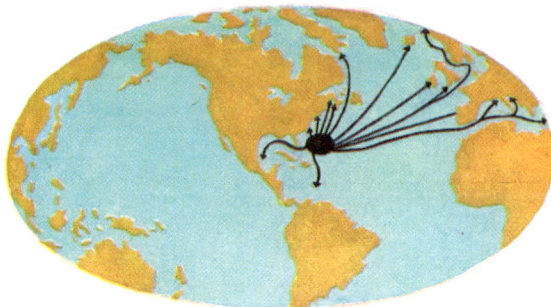

in almost the same area of the Sargasso Sea. The shorter return voyage of the American leptocephali, which is also shown on the map, means that they grow much faster than their trans-Atlantic cousins, and their journey takes

33

only one year. Among all the mysteries of the sea, few have aroused more speculation than the three-thousand mile journey of the adult European eel, and the three-year return journey of the baby eels to their ancestral habitats.

THE ROCK CLINGER

As the first rays of the early summer sun lights their village, a group of Maoris set off to go fishing for the **lamprey**. This remarkable animal, when hatched, lives in sandy shallow backwaters near the banks of rivers, and differs considerably in appearance from the adults. When it reaches a length of three inches, it undergoes a transformation, and begins to move down river, on its journey to the sea. The lamprey remains feeding in the sea, until it reaches its full length of about a foot. It then begins its long journey back, re-entering the rivers in brightly coloured shoals, and is now considered a special delicacy. The lamprey travels upstream until its way is finally barred by rocks, and it is to these that it clings with its sucker-like mouth. Here certain Maoris, selected by tribal position and tradition, come to catch their easy prey, returning in triumph to their villages in the evening with the spoils. Lampreys are not true fishes but primitive vertebrates. The remains of their ancestors are found in rocks nearly four hundred million years old. Most lampreys have a sucker-like mouth at the front end of their eel-like body. This New Zealand lamprey has, in addition, a large bag almost obscuring the mouth. Nobody knows what the purpose of this bag might be, and to say the least it is a quite unusual and remarkable structure, unlike anything found in other species of lamprey.

New Zealand lamprey (*Geotria australis*)

THE PRIZE OF THE MOUNTAINS

One of the most sought-after prizes is the elusive **Parnassius butterfly** which has led collectors on tiring treks up the highest moun-

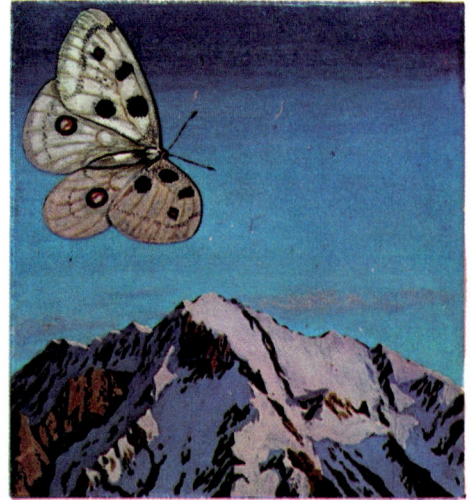

Alpine butterfly (*Parnassius* sp.)

tains of Europe, Asia and America. One species ranges into the Arctic, and only one, the Apollo butterfly, flies at low altitudes. The Parnassius is essentially an alpine butterfly. Its body is covered with hairs, like a fur coat, and is dark-coloured to absorb the heat of the sun. The body is also smaller in proportion to the size of the wings, as compared with most other butterflies, and it is suggested that this exposes a proportionately greater surface for the absorption of heat from the sun. The wings, moreover, are so thinly covered with scales as to be almost translucent, which would also aid in the absorption of heat. As might be expected a Parnassius butterfly cannot tolerate the onset of winter and goes into hibernation. Living under these cold conditions the rate of growth of a Parnassius is very slow since the warm life-giving summers are so short. Thus it spends a large part of its life asleep, and it takes as long as two years to reach maturity.

FAR-FLYING MONARCH

Have you ever wondered what happens to a beautiful butterfly when summer ends and its filmy wings are seen no more fluttering among the flowers? Some butterflies live for only a few days or weeks, and others sleep through numbering tens of thousands are seen flying over great cities like New York and San Francisco. When March brings spring again, the black-and-brown banded butterflies drift north again, but they are more scattered as compared with the southward journey. Individual monarch butterflies have reached as far as Australia and Formosa to the west, and to England and the European Continent to the east, but nobody is sure whether such migrants have flown these tremendous distances under their own power, or have been carried on ships. But since this far-flying migrant has been sighted flying five hundred miles out at sea, it is a fair bet that it spans the vast oceans on its own wings.

THE GLOBE TROTTERS

No doubt the greatest insect travellers in the world are colourful butterflies known as **painted ladies,** so-called for their bright and distinctive wings. They can be found not only in all temperate parts of the world, but on every continent except South America. Whenever a place becomes too populated, an adventurous group will branch off and migrate to a new territory and form a colony there. The entire species roves twice yearly to find warm winters in the south and comfortable summers in the north, flying as fast as sixteen miles an hour. Most remarkable, though, are the tremendous distances they can cover without stopping. For instance, they will travel from Europe to Africa, across the Mediterranean, three hundred to five hundred miles, or from Australia to New Zealand, one thousand miles, or even from California to Hawaii, more than two thousand miles, incredible distances for fragile creatures only two and one half inches from wing to wing, who seem to have an incurable wanderlust.

BY-THE-WIND-SAILOR

On most of the earth's warm seas can be seen a small violet-blue jellyfish, which hoists its own tiny sail to navigate the ocean. The **Velella jellyfish,** which has been given the name By-the-wind-sailor, has a transparent, paper-thin sail on top of a two-inch wide float, which is rendered buoyant by the gas-filled chambers it contains. It is, however, unable to deflate this in order to submerge when a storm threatens. Only in the larval stage is it able to do this. Swarms of Velella bob along on the water with their little sails hoisted, and underneath the

Monarch butterfly (*Danaus plexippus*)

the winter in some sheltered nook. But some hardy butterflies fly great distances to spend winter in warm climates. Such a sturdy creature is the big, red-brown **monarch butterfly** of the northern United States and southern Canada, which flies to warm southern states, and even to Mexico and the Caribbean. When the first autumn winds blow, in September, the monarch butterfly joins its fellows for their great southward migration. Sometimes swarms

Painted lady (*Vanessa cardui*)

THE LUMINESCENT WANDERER

As the great ocean liner ploughs through the silent night, its sharp bow cleaving the still waters, the passengers eagerly crowd the rail. They are straining for a glimpse of a great shoal of **Pelagia**, a luminescent jellyfish. From the distance it looks like a host of tiny winking spots of light, quite different from the even glow of the single-celled protozoans, those other luminescent denizens of the ocean. As the ship draws nearer the winking lights begin to look like thousands of balls of bluish fire, floating at the surface. This effect is caused by the jellyfish's luminescent umbrella, about two inches across. Drifting with the ocean currents on journeys covering vast distances, the Pelagia is swept up the American coast by the Gulf Stream and eastwards by the North Atlantic Current. Indeed, the very same jelly-fishes that entertain children on the shores of Western Scotland may have previously entertained other children thousands of miles away on the coast of the United States.

THE SHORT-TRIP PAIR

In contrast to the many animals that migrate long distances each year, some make only short trips. One of these is the two-foot long **horseshoe crab**. There are several species of these which live in waters about sixty feet deep off the coasts of Japan, from Japan through the seas off China to the Malay Peninsula, and off eastern North America. *Limulus polyphemus* is the American species. This sword-tailed creature is not really a crab at all, but a relative of the spiders. Each summer male and female travel towards the shore where the

float dangle numerous light-blue stinging tentacles, used to catch food. When the winds persist from one quarter for a long time, and the seas remain fairly calm, Velella is carried inexorably towards the coast, and it is then we see thousands upon thousands of them cast up on the beaches, unable to help themselves.

Velella jellyfish (*Velella spirans*)

Luminescent jellyfish (*Pelagia noctiluca*)

Horseshoe crab (*Limulus polyphemus*)

female lays her eggs in shallow waters. The male accompanies her on their annual expedition, grasping the end of her dark-green domed shell, and gently pushing her along. At several places in the shallow waters the female stops, thrusts her eight-inch wide body about two inches into the sand, and lays about a thousand eggs each time. When their trip is finished, the horseshoe crab pair return to the deeper water, and there, until next summer, they spend most of their time scooping their way through the sand and mud of the ocean bottom, hunting for worms and shell-less molluscs.

THE FIRST PHALANGER

The **cuscus** was the first of the Australian animals to be called Phalanger, which could be roughly translated as "the fingered one". This is an allusion to the shape of the animal's fingers and toes, especially the toes on the hind-feet, which can be used to grasp branches in climbing. The cuscus belongs to the possum family whose members are found only in the forests of Queensland, in Australia, and the neighbouring island of New Guinea. Only the males have spotted fur, the females being a uniform brownish-grey, although in a species on the island of Waigiou, off New Guinea, both sexes are spotted. This is not surprising because cuscuses do vary more than usual in

New Guinea spotted cuscus *(Phalanger maculatus)*

THE FINGERY ONE

Tap-tap-tap, the long sensitive fingers of the **striped phalanger** strike the bark of a rotten stump. Then, after sniffing about with its sensitive nostrils, it tears the wood apart with its sharp, curved front teeth. The name Phalanger "the fingered one" is applicable to this black-and-white animal in another way. Having gnawed a hole in the wood it inserts its long, naked middle finger which is twice as long as the others and shaped like a spoon. Extracting the grubs with this finger it then picks them up with its tongue. Found in the Queensland province of Australia, the striped phalanger, a good tree-climber, lives in the deeper forested sections. The long, soft fur is patterned like that of a skunk, and like the skunks the striped phalanger can give out a strong unpleasant odour, although it does not squirt a fluid as they do.

the pattern and colour of the coat, and also in the colour of the eyes, which may be brown, black, red or blue. Cuscuses spend the day curled up in the fork of a tree, and if they move at all they are slow and sloth-like. At night they become active and they eat large quantities of leaves, but they will also eat lizards and small mammals, as well as birds and their eggs. The ears are small and half-hidden in the fur, but if their hearing is poor their sight at night is good.

1. **Grey ring-tailed possum**
(Pseudochirus peregrinus)
2. **Brush-tailed or vulpine possum**
(Trichosurus vulpecula)
3. **Tasmanian or dusky brush-tailed phalanger**
(Trichosurus fuliginosus)
4. **Short-eared brush-tailed possum**
(Trichosurus caninus)

Striped phalanger
(Dactylopsila picata)

A QUARTET FROM "DOWN-UNDER"

There is some doubt whether it was the famous explorer Captain Cook or the scientist, Sir Joseph Banks, who accompanied him on one of his visits to Australia, who called these animals "opossums" because of their resemblance to the North American animals of that name. Since that time Australians have dropped the first letter and called them "possums". Harmless vegetarians, these four possums live mainly in holes in trees, only venturing out at night to feed on leaves, fruit and nuts, using the hairless strip on the underside of the tail to help in gripping the branches. The **brush-tailed** or **vulpine possum** is found in most parts of Australia, is fox-like in size and has a fox-like head. It may be found on treeless plains living in old rabbit burrows or at the very top of a tall gum tree. The **short-eared brushtail** keeps to high, densely wooded regions. It is hunted for its fur, which, although valuable, is not as spectacular as that of its cousin, the **Tasmanian** or **dusky brushtail** which owes its gorgeous colouring to the fact that the colour varies from blackish-brown or grey to reddish or golden amber, the last of these being a partial albino. The **grey ring-tailed possum** derives its name from the way the tail is carried coiled at the end.

THE OLD MAN AND HIS MOB

The comparative quiet of the open forest country of Southern Australia is broken by a scuffling, thumping commotion. A large party of **great grey kangaroos,** proceeding on their way in tremendous leaps and bounds of up to twenty-five feet at a time, has decided to stop, while the leader, known as the "Old Man" or "Boomer" deals with an insubordinate younger male who has challenged his authority. Determined to maintain his domi-

1. **Great grey kangaroo** (*Macropus major*)
2. **Red kangaroo** (*Macropus rufus*)

nant position in the mob against wild "youngsters" in the ranks, the "guvnor" stages a kind of boxing match and proceeds to set about the offender. It does not take long for the fight to develop; the two kangaroos engage in a lively display of furry fisticuffs – ignoring a few rules of the game by biting and barging, while the dust flies around them. Suddenly the "Old

Young of the red kangaroo

Man" deals his shattering knock-out blow; with a terrific down-cut of one of his hind-feet he delivers his coup de grace – and another kangaroo bites the dust of defeat. The **red kangaroo,** living on the open plains, also travels about in "mobs" under the watchful and paternal eye of an older male, exercising his authority in the same way and not hesitating to use his mighty-muscled tail. When considering these athletic displays and the size of the participants, it is surprising to find that the young kangaroo is only one inch long at birth, while in comparison to this insignificant length the adult can be as tall as seven feet. The young one shelters and is fed out of sight in the mother's pouch until it is about four months old, then, warily it pokes out its head and begins to feed on grass as the mother wanders about. As it grows and becomes stronger, it will venture out beside her, but will very quickly return to and take refuge in the pouch if alarmed or frightened. Kangaroos are not very intelligent and when panicked these large, likeable creatures will rush into headlong flight, make all the wrong moves, run around in circles, trip

over their own companions and sometimes knock themselves out by crashing headlong into walls or fences or other similar immovable obstacles. But the likeable character and appearance of the kangaroo still make it a world favourite with children and adults everywhere.

A TREE KANGAROO

You hardly expect to see a kangaroo up a tree, but this one actually sleeps aloft. His ancestors were probably ground wallabies that later took to the trees, probably for security. In fact, the **tree kangaroo** is also quite happy on the ground, feeding on leaves, ferns, and almost any kind of fruit. Its tail was possibly once prehensile, capable of grasping, but it is not relatively as powerful as that of the common kangaroo, and is now used entirely for balancing. For a tree-climber it is awkward when descending, coming down tail-first. If alarmed, it will jump directly down from heights of 60 feet or more. It often lives alone, a solitary forager, or in small families in rocky or hilly districts of Queensland.

The Aborigines hunt tree kangaroos with dogs. Several of them will climb into the trees and drive the kangaroos down, or make them jump, to the dogs waiting below.

Tree kangaroo (*Dendrolagus* sp.)

Western hare wallaby (*Lagorchestes hirsutus*)

THE SMALLEST KANGAROO

On rare occasions in Western Australia, when travelling in the outback, a very small, less than two foot high, kangaroo-like creature with the physical aspects and looks of a hare may be seen. The **hare wallaby** has slender, pointed ears, immense hind legs with narrow feet, and a slim tail. Everything about this animal, the smallest of the Kangaroo family, is streamlined, and adapted for high speed and incredible feats of jumping. This brown-backed and clear-fronted wallaby is nocturnal, sleeping in "forms" or "seats" similar to hares, during the day. Completely defenceless, this mammal is now becoming rare, as a result of the large numbers of European animals, such as foxes and domesticated cats and dogs, introduced into Australia, which prey on it. Hare wallabies are reputed to make clear jumps of eight to ten feet when hotly pressed. The naturalist Gould told of one being chased by dogs that doubled back and, finding him in its path, jumped clean over his head.

THE ROCK POLISHER

The sound of steady thumping was heard among the rocks, a number of kangaroo-like heads lifted in alarm, as the "danger approaching" signal was heard. With one accord they all turned and began a headlong dash for safety. Leaping over and among the rocks, with the practised ease of performing acrobats, they made their way to the shelter and security of their cave homes. The **rock wallabies** are slender animals with long hindlegs and feet and long furred tails. They thump on the ground with the hind-feet to signal alarm, much as the rabbit does. The tail is used as a rudder when jumping. Living exclusively in hilly country, they feed on grass, foliage, bark and roots. The wallabies' life follows a routine. They live, feed, and rear their families in the same areas year after year, generation after generation. That is why, leading to their cave haunts, there is an almost polished path across the rock face, shone by countless numbers of padded feet. The soles of the feet are granulated.

AN UNPLEASANT CUSTOMER

The **solenodon** of Cuba, looks like an enormous coarsely-furred rat. The long nose is somewhat grotesque, looking like the tapering end of a parsnip-root sprouting long, ever-quivering hairs. These hairs are probably more sensitive than a cat's whiskers, and are used in the search for food. The solenodon is not particular about what it eats, but goes for anything available, including lizards, the larger insects, dead birds or other carrion. When sitting up to lick its fur or to eat, it squats on the hind-feet and tail, like a kangaroo. When walking the curvature of its claws compels it to walk on "tip-toe". It is credited with a thoroughly vile temper, and is subject to outbursts of fury, when it will let out hellish screams, and snap viciously at anything within reach. There is a second species, *Solenodon paradoxus*, on the island of Haiti. It also is about a foot long and nocturnal, resting by day in hollow logs or among rocks. Both species are distantly related to hedgehogs and shrews.

Ringed-tail rock wallaby *(Petrogale xanthopus)*

Solenodon *(Solenodon cubanus)*

MADAGASCAR'S RING-TAIL

South of Madagascars's Morondava River, in the very dry southern tip of the island, dwell the lovely **ring-tailed lemurs.** Most lemurs live in forests, but the ring-tails differ from them in inhabiting the dry, rocky and thinly-wooded country. Found in groups, they scamper about the rocks and scrublands on all fours, but never take to the trees. Unlike other lemurs, the ring-tail has palms that are long, smooth and leatherlike. Its grip on even a wet slippery rock is so sure that it is able to walk up it like a fly moving up a pane of glass. The search for food takes place during the morning and early evening hours. The ring-tail seems to be wholly vegetarian, eating wild bananas, roots, and the fruit of a cactus. Night-time as well as the hottest part of the day is sleeping time. This soft-furred, grey-and-white animal rests on a rock with its long ringed, furry tail wrapped round its neck. Although loud and

Ring-tailed lemur *(Lemur catta)*

noisy with its catlike calls while out hunting, when resting the ring-tail utters just a few contented "hoo" sounds.

THE SPEAR THROWER

The **indri,** related to that odd family of animals, the lemurs, but in a separate family from them, wanders in large groups through the volcanic mountains of Madagascar. It has only a two-inch stump of a tail at the end of its two-foot-long body. Swinging by its large hairy hands and feet (it looks as if it is wearing woolly gloves) the indri moves rapidly through the tree-tops feeding on leaves, fruit and shoots. Possessing highly-developed hands, like man, it eats by lifting food to the mouth. Its cries also recall a suffering human in distress and if wounded will fall to the ground yelling and screaming so loudly as to make the hunter regret having harmed it. This behaviour has caused the natives of Madagascar to name the indri the "forest dog", and to regard it with superstition. They tell many legends of the indri's prodigious feats, including one that credits it with the ability to catch a spear thrown at it and hurl it back at the hunter.

Indri *(Indri indri)* ➡

44

THE SUNBATHER

As dawn was breaking in the forest of Madagascar and the animal kingdom prepared to meet another day, a little mischievous black face with a white muzzle, and a white ruff round its ears and throat, peered expectantly towards the east. As the sun rose majestically over the horizon, the **ruffed lemur,** fixing its eyes on the ball of fire, slowly raised its arms, as if in prayer and supplication. The largest of the lemurs, it is three feet long, including the tail, a handsome social animal, that travels in large groups through the branches chattering incessantly as it browses on leaves, buds and fruit. When in high spirits the ruffed lemur will chase small birds through the branches in a breath-taking display of acrobatic agility, its long tail, used as a balancer, flowing out behind. This hectic dash will come to a sudden halt for refreshment if the lemur sees a nest containing

Ruffed lemur or maki *(Lemur variegatus)*

pigmies look for a hole in a tree. There the babies, usually twins, are born, so tiny their fingers cannot be seen without a magnifying-glass. Even so, they are never tied to mother's apron-strings for, oddly enough, it is father who carries them around, one tucked into each groin. He hands them over to mother only when feeding-time comes around.

A BLOOD-CURDLING SCREAM

Through the canopy-like foliage of the Central American jungle swings a troupe of **black howlers,** their black silky fur glinting in the dappled sunlight. Using all four feet and their prehensile tails they move through the tree-tops faster than a man can move along the ground. Suddenly they halt, and the leader, a large male, sends a blood-curdling, ear-shattering scream echoing round the green vaults, a sound that, once heard by a human being, is never forgotten. This cry, produced by two bony sound-box structures inside his throat, is the howler's way of warning other troupes to keep off his feeding territory. He starts with a low growl, changing first into a series of booming howls and then into a racket which has been compared to four jaguars fighting together. The black howler may

Pigmy marmoset (*Cebuella pygmaea*)

eggs. The ruffed lemur is the only variety of common type of lemur to build a nest of its own, which is occupied by the whole family. Ruffed lemurs may be bright red or black-and-white.

SMALLEST MONKEY

The sun beats fiercely down on the tangled vegetation of Brazil's equatorial forests. There, under a leafy canopy formed by the tallest trees, exists a great variety of animal life seen nowhere else in the world. One, for example, is a rat-sized animal known as the **pigmy marmoset,** six inches in head and body length, the smallest of the true monkeys. Its "pop" eyes and round head remind one of a Pekinese puppy. Its fur is so fine that one's finger-tip can scarcely feel it. It lives high up, like a penthouse dweller in a skyscraper, but as it is quite comfortable clinging to a tree trunk no nest is needed. Only during the breeding season do these

Black howler (*Alouatta caraya*)

sometimes be seen hanging upside-down by its tail from a tree branch, feeding on fruit and leaves, with an incongruously melancholy expression on its face.

GARDEN RAIDER

The smallest of the African monkeys, the **pygmy guenon,** is a native of the Congo. It is always to be found high up in the trees on a river bank, and usually near a village, where it causes havoc by stealing crops, usually the most succulent ones, and corn, stuffing huge quantities of fruit into its **cheek-pouches** to carry away and eat later. After a raid it dashes off through the trees, swinging nimbly among the branches to the river bank where the chattering "tribe" is assembled. Even as an adult the pygmy guenon has a baby-face, with a permanently surprised expression. Like most monkeys, it delights in throwing things, sending a cascade of half-eaten fruits on the heads of the **harassed African gardeners,** and accompanying all this with its "plish, plish" call – like the sound of a stick being thrown into water.

SEASHORE MONKEY BUSINESS

If you think monkeys live only in trees or jungles, here is a surprise! Meet our friend from Formosa who lives along the rocky seashore, makes his home in caves, and thinks nothing of diving into the water to fish up a succulent crab. It is not because there are no trees to live in, for just a few miles inland this island home abounds in rich forests, and yet this monkey prefers the seashore. No doubt, a long way back, its ancestors accidentally discovered how delicious crab could be and in pursuit of this new-found delicacy developed into good swimmers, which is unusual, for most monkeys avoid water. Very shy, the **Formosan macaque** spends most of the day solitary in a cave and at twilight joins its fellows, in small groups, to comb the shore for berries, tender shoots of plants, grasshoppers and, above all, their favourite shellfish. This seashore oddity is a comedian who needs no audience. Looking, from a distance, like a little old man with his beard and whiskers, he will often sit for hours on a rock by himself, chattering away and crying, apparently for his own amusement.

ANOTHER BREAST-STROKE SWIMMER

The theory has been put forward in recent years that the human species once lived an aquatic

Pygmy guenon or talapoin *(Cercopithecus talapoin)*

life. This theory has not been generally accepted by scientists, and it is of interest to consider it in the light of what has just been written here about the Formosan macaque. When we look around the animal kingdom we find remarkably few land animals that cannot swim if really put to it. Some, like the grey squirrel, the stoat and the deer, will often swim, either to cross a river or a lake. Snakes will swim; hedgehogs and badgers will take to the water; foxes and hares will swim a river when being pursued. Even an ostrich will swim. All these use the same movements in swimming as they use when moving about on land. The Formosan macaque, however, uses a breast-stroke, quite unlike its locomotion on land. The Indian macaque, will sometimes swim – breast-stroke. And this is the "natural" method for human beings to swim.

LAST OF THE FOREST MANDARINS

Behind the great wall of swamp forests fringing the western coasts of Borneo and Sumatra, isolated colonies of **orang-utans** cling to their ancient way of life among the trees, the old rules and customs still observed. Here the **great apes sit quietly or move slowly through the branches, feeding on fruit, leaves and bark, crunching their food with enormous biting jaws.** Remarkably meditative and calm in appearance, young orang-utans look soulful; the adults, especially the old males, seem to be full of ancient, sorrowful wisdom. But the high, broad forehead and intensely human expression of these venerable patriarchs belie their enormous **strength** and agility. Although deliberate in their movements and extremely cautious, orang-utans can travel faster through the trees than men can move over the ground. They have been seen to make great leaps outwards and downwards from the soaring tops of tall trees to the massed foliage of lower tree tops – their enormous arms, stretching eight feet from hand to hand, spread wide as they hurtle bodily through space sixty feet above the ground. But for the most part, these great apes sit quietly in the untroubled silence of their leafy world, the huge pouches on their cheeks sagging as if with the weight of old sorrow. And well they may, for unless protective measures can be successfully pressed home, this grand Old Man of the Woods, isolated in this corner of the world, may soon be a thing of the past.

THE ORANG-UTAN COULD NOT SWIM

When we look at the Old Man of the Woods we realize that he would make a poor show at swimming. Not only would his long hair be a serious handicap when it became water-logged, as much a handicap as when a man has to swim in his clothes, but his arms are too long and his legs too weak. The orang-utan feeds mainly on fruit, but it also has been known to go to

Formosan macaque (*Macaca cyclopis*)

Orang-utan *(Pongo pygmaeus)*

the seashore and eat shellfish, so the orang-utan has been known to go near water, but has never been seen to swim. If you try to swim breaststroke using only your arms not only do you make little progress but your body soon begins to sink and you find yourself upright in the water, struggling to keep afloat. The legs provide, therefore, the main propulsive force. The orang-utan, the gorilla and chimpanzee, the gibbon, and many monkeys, have arms much longer than their legs. This is one reason why most of them avoid water.

ALONE IN THE FOREST

Ambling through the deepening gloom of the rain forests of equatorial Africa, the old silverbacked **gorilla** swings his huge bulk along on his feet and the knuckles of great hands – his big head turning perhaps a little uneasily on massive shoulders. At last he settles and makes himself a bed for the night of leaves and branches. At the foot of a tall tree he looks shorter than six feet tall because of his vast bulk – he weighs more than six hundred pounds. As darkness begins to gather through the forest,

Gorilla *(Gorilla gorilla)*

he can hear the sounds of a family party
settling down for the night – the mothers
cradling their young in the security of the
platform nests constructed in the trees; the
male gorilla on guard below. Although
gorillas usually go about in family parties of
one mature male with several females and their
young, occasionally a male will be driven out
or may elect to go off on his own. A light rain
begins to filter down through the high canopy
of the forest, and this solitary old bull stares out
from beneath his heavy brows into the darkness. Gorillas do not like rain, and this one has
a lost, lonely expression – almost the look of
an elderly outcast. It could serve as a symbol
for the entire race of great apes which seems
doomed to extinction. For despite their great
size and strength, and their shy, almost docile
behaviour, evolution seems to have passed
them by, leaving them alone in a deepening
darkness. They feed on the ground, on vegeta-
ation only, mainly wild celery, bamboo shoots
and berries. They are not expert climbers, like
the orang-utan, but they can swing their heavy
bodies up to the lower branches of low trees.
The females and youngsters sometimes take
to the trees when confronted by danger, while
the bull gorilla covers their retreat – rising to
his full height and glaring savagely at the
intruder. If this does not scare away the attacker,

he pounds the vast drum of his chest with his open hands and utters a series of deep guttural noises. If the attacker turns and retreats, he may pursue it, but usually he stands his ground, satisfied to be left in peace; and after a while he moves on, to follow the females and young.

Capable of ripping the shoulder from a leopard with one blow of his hand, his great size and strength protect him against all predators except man. Yet the gorilla is essentially peaceful, and will not attack unless provoked. Young gorillas are, however, sometimes preyed on by leopards, usually when they stray from

Black ape of Celebes (*Cynopithecus niger*)

the family group. As intelligent as the tree-dwelling primates, the gorilla is not as mechanically inclined nor as playful as the orang-utan or chimpanzee, but young gorillas are as appealing as any young mammal, tumbling and crawling about over their mothers, and full of curiosity about the world around. Even a snake seems to do no more than excite their curiosity. Weaned at the end of the first year, gorillas reach maturity when they are between ten and twelve years old. An old gorilla may live to be thirty years of age, but it seems that he stays in exile after having been successfully challenged by a younger male. Young but mature males also leave the family group to lead solitary lives, and it is believed now that they do this until strong enough to return and challenge an old male.

FATHER OF THE TRIBE

Primitive man has from time immemorial felt a close kinship to wild animals and has often adopted the bravest or fiercest as the emblem of the tribe. The indigenous people of the coastal regions of the island of Celebes have claimed descent from one of the strangest of the world's monkeys – the so-called **black ape of Celebes.** This baboon-like monkey is a gentle creature, who lives in the coastal mangrove forests. Here he feeds on fruit and leaves and hunts for sea-food along the lonely beaches. A shy, retiring animal covered with thick black fur, he has the long, dog-like muzzle of a baboon with prominent brows and odd swellings in the cheeks. But his most extraordinary feature is his crest of stiff hairs atop his head which can be erected at will – giving him a most peculiar appearance. No one knows his history, since he has no close

Capybara (*Hydrochoerus hydrochaeris*) ➤

Black-tailed jack rabbit (*Lepus californicus*)

relatives among the animals we know as primates. He is not a baboon nor is he an ape. He is, in fact, unique.

THE LONG EARED JUMPER

At the stealthy approach of the two children the **black-tailed jack rabbit's** ears twitch like two fingers. In a second it leaps from behind the tangle of briar bush across the path. In one jump it covers twenty feet. In another it is caught only momentarily in the beam of sunlight filtering through the trees before it disappears entirely from view. This black-tailed jack rabbit does not have to keep to the undergrowth for protection like some of its smaller relatives. Its long and powerful legs make a fast getaway an easy affair. They call it the Antelope Hare, which is a tribute to its speed. It is said to run and jump over miles of rough terrain at speeds reaching at times forty-five miles an hour – a speed difficult for an antelope or even a greyhound to equal. This jack rabbit, makes its home in the grassy uninhabited meadows of the Western United States and in the stately redwood forests of California.

THE DIGNIFIED RODENT

The **capybara** is the largest living rodent, reaching a length of up to four feet and a weight of 120 pounds. In addition to its large size, which has earned it the name of water pig, it is unlike the usual run of rodents in many other ways. It lives in groups, always near water and, if undisturbed, spends its time complacently chewing water plants or grass, or maize and other cultivated crops. When alarmed it runs in the manner of a horse, but it readily takes to water, and can swim for long distances under water, using its webbed feet. Its enemies include the jaguar on land and the caiman in the water, and against these it has no defence. In captivity it is inoffensive and readily tamed. Most rodent females nurse their young lying down. The female capybara stands to suckle her young, which usually number two but may be as many as eight, and are well-developed at birth.

OUR DISTANT RELATIVE

The island of Borneo – like the island of Madagascar – is the home of many strange animals. One of the most intriguing of these is the **tree-shrew**, or "Tupai" as it is called by the Malaysian-speaking peoples of the island. This word rhymes with "two pie" and simply means any

Tree-shrew (*Tupaia tana*)

fast-moving squirrel-like animal that lives in trees. Indeed, with its long bushy tail it looks very like the squirrels living in the same trees. The tree-shrew, however, has a long shrew-like snout and the vicious, quarrelsome temper of the shrew for whom it is named in the English language. It was formerly classified with the shrews, but is now placed with the lemurs, and is of special interest to human beings, since some scientists believe it to be a distant relative of ours. It has a tiny appendix like ours, five fingers and five toes, and sits upright when it eats – holding its dinner in its hands. It also has what must be one of the more striking human characteristics: it is very fond of water and

Asian dwarf squirrel (*Nannosciurus* sp.)

takes a regular bath in rain-filled hollows in the trees. This is most unusual among mammals.

PIGMY PARACHUTIST

In the matted canopy of the forests of Malaya and Borneo scampers the smallest of the world's squirrels, the **Asian dwarf squirrel.** Not much bigger than a three-inch mouse, it is shown here beside a rupee, the small coin of India. This timid olive-green creature compensates for its small size by having disproportionately large teeth, with which it easily cracks and chews the smaller nuts and berries growing in abundance in its tree-top habitat. It never builds a nest for itself, as many squirrels do, but sleeps in hollows in trees, or even far out on swaying branches. The Asian dwarf squirrel is an amusing sight as it streaks from tree to tree in flying leaps, using its bushy tail as a rudder to steer right or left, or as a parachute, once it has launched itself amid the tree-tops.

THE ANIMATED CACTUS

Unaware that it is stalking an animated cactus, the farm dog circles the bristling ball. The **crested porcupine** stamps a warning with its feet and mutters and growls as it rattles its quills. Carefully, out of curiosity, the dog sniffs as the porcupine spins nimbly about, exposing only its spiny rump. Suddenly the porcupine runs backwards, driving its quills into the dog's face. These come away as easily as dry Christmas tree needles and embed themselves firmly in the dog's nose. A wiser dog could have called its bluff, for although the quills are formidable, the porcupine's head is covered only with long flexible bristles and is very vulnerable. Having disposed of its enemy, the crested porcupine resumes its gnawing of the axe handle, attracted by the salt deposited on it by perspiring hands. Its jaws, stronger than those of any other herbivorous mammal, soon cut the wood in two. Then the porcupine ambles off through the night, grunting and grinding its teeth, in search of appetising roots. This arrogant but stupid animal, the largest of the porcupine family, measuring twenty-eight inches long, is found in Italy, Sicily, part of the Balkans, North Africa and West Africa.

ALL NIGHT EATER

A good-tempered dweller in the mighty tropical forests of South America is the tree-porcupine known as the **coendou.** It is smaller and lighter in weight than ground porcupines, and

Common or crested porcupine (*Hystrix cristata*)

is covered with short, close spines intermixed with hair. Its greatest advantage over ground porcupines is a remarkably long prehensile tail. With the tip of its tail almost automatically curling round any branch it touches, the coendou indulges in tree travel without fear of slipping. During the day it holes up in any cavity it can find in a tree trunk or hollowed-out log. Night-time is eating time, and it roams in a leisurely fashion, for food is plentiful, and no

Coendou (*Coendou prehensilis*)

exertion is needed to find it. All around are leaves, the barks of trees and bushes, nuts, and many sorts of fruit. From the moment it wakes until daylight sends it home to rest, the coendou's time is spent in almost ceaseless nibbling and gnawing. As with all rodents, this is a dental necessity, for the gnawing teeth, or incisors, are growing constantly from their roots and must be constantly worn down at their cutting edges.

COON UP A TREE

High in the Himalaya mountains, west of Nepal to China and south to Laos, lives an extraordinary raccoon-like animal related to the giant panda. The **lesser panda** has the same endear-

Lesser panda (*Ailurus fulgens*)

ing pigeon-toed walk and smooth bear-like fur as its larger relative, but sports an enormous bushy tail. Trundling along on soft paws, it forages on the ground, selecting choice leaves from the hardy mountain plants, but it is otherwise an arboreal animal – spending most of its time in the trees. As with some other mammals, the parents in this unique species of panda live together at all times and are usually followed by a line of young ones of various sizes. A closely knit family, the lesser pandas do not welcome visitors, and are apt to become testy when annoyed.

Spotted skunk *(Spilogale putorius)*

SPOTTED SKUNK

Just under two feet long when full-grown, the **spotted skunk** is as indifferent to the presence of other animals and of men as its white-striped brother from the north. "Spotted" is hardly an apt description since its body is marked with irregular stripes that may in places be broken into spots. With its conspicuous coloration acting as a warning to be respected, this many-striped species is readily granted the right of way by most of its carnivorous neighbours. Once a hawk was observed flying away with a small skunk in its talons. Using its very loose skin to squirm into position, the skunk fired its foul-smelling spray at its captor. Instantly dropping the skunk, the hawk flew erratically away, wildly shaking its head. At feeding time, one can see this awkward, rather square-built animal cautiously sniffing the

Sloth bear *(Melursus ursinus)* ➡

Malayan sun bear *(Helarctos malayanus)*

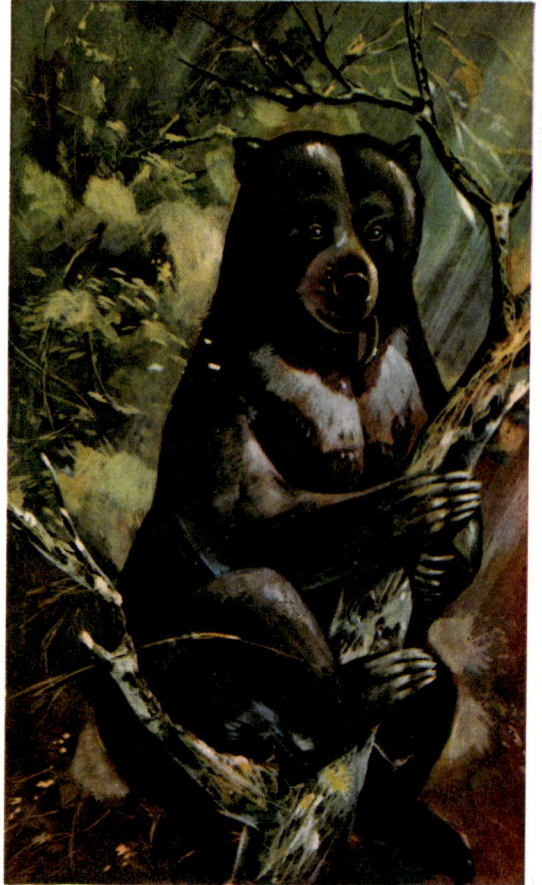

A SUNNY DISPOSITION

The **Malayan sun bear** looks down with its usual benign expression at the group of monkeys playing on the ground. Its coarse hair glistens in the intense rays of light that filter through the trees, where it has stationed itself to receive as much of the pleasantly warming sun as possible. Suddenly the monkeys chatter wildly and scatter up the nearby trees. The Malayan sun bear is also, lethargically, moved to action. It is, however, too heavy and too cumbersome to raise its four and a half foot bulk any higher in the tree. Instead it ambles down from its perch to escape across the ground. Into the jungle clearing come two men with nets and ropes. Soon the bear is thoroughly entangled. They put it into a large basket to carry into the town where it will be sold as a pet. It is common to see this animal chained behind the gates of sumptuous estates. The Malayan sun bear, the smallest of all bears, well-known for its amiable disposition, as well as its fondness for honey and syrup, is found from the east Himalayas and Sze Chwan in China south to Burma and Malaya, and the islands of Sumatra and Borneo.

ground as it works its way into the undergrowth. Rooting with its snout, this native of the United States seeks out grasshoppers, and other insects. It also eats mice, rats and birds.

TERMITE TERROR

The **sloth bear,** of India and Ceylon, has very shaggy fur, particularly on the neck and flanks. It lumbers from branch to branch through the forests like an upside-down version of a bear walking a high wire. The one in the background has found a heavy old branch which it rips apart with its long claws. In a few minutes it has raised a cloud of dust and wood particles. Termites from the nest in the stump scatter in all directions as the bear's long tongue and sensitive lips search through the huge nest for the insects and their larvae. It will also blow away the dust and pick up the insects with its mobile lips which, exceptionally among bears, are almost completely naked. Having cleaned out the nest thoroughly, the sloth bear again shuffles off, again clinging upside-down to the branches. This time it is after some grapes, to which it reaches out with its long tongue. It needs soft foods because it has only weak teeth.

RIVER DOLPHIN

The passengers on the steamer up the Irrawaddy river, were admiring the early morning view, when they were entertained by a large school of dolphins, each about seven feet long and black in colour, swimming in front of and alongside the steamer, and leaping out of the water one after another, like a well-trained group of aquatic acrobats. The **Irrawaddy dolphin,** like the dolphins and porpoises living in the sea, seem to take pleasure in swimming in the bow-waves of ships, acting as escort and pilot to the steamers going up and down the Irrawaddy for a thousand miles. It has tiny eyes and a small downward pointing mouth, with lips that come together in a point in front. Its small flippers are placed far forward, its tail flukes are large and the dorsal fin is small. It feeds on crayfish, fresh-water snails and shrimps, which it finds by grubbing about on the muddy bed of the river. It never leaves the water, but one is shown here on the bank in order to illustrate its shape.

THE DISAPPEARING SEAL

The most famous performing seal in the world is the **California sea-lion.** It differs from the true seals in having ears and in being able to

Irrawaddy dolphin *(Orcaella brevirostris)*

move over the ground using its front flippers, but it is so smooth and sleek-headed that it looks to most of us exactly what a seal should be like. Its value as a circus animal is due to a natural ability to balance things on its nose, a skill it often uses in the wild, for this sea-lion has been seen to rise straight up in the water and toss fish in the air before swallowing them. It also has the trick of remaining submerged when hunting sea-gulls. Only its pointed nose twitches above the waves and unwary gulls, attracted by this lure, swoop down and are quickly gobbled up. The Farallone islands off the California coast are the main breeding grounds for the California sea-lion. Every May these rocky islands are covered with thousands of barking and howling males, each capturing or enticing as many females as possible into its harem. The clamour set up by these enormous colonies continues through the summer until the pups, born usually in June, are weaned in September. Then the great herds slip back beneath the waves and move south, leaving the islands like abandoned camp-sites in the cold and fog of winter. Not until next spring will the islands echo to the joyous barking of the world's favourite performing seal.

AN INFLATABLE TRUNK

This giant of the seal family, derives its name from the long, fleshy "trunk" the male, or bull, sports on his snout. This trunk is an enormous snout, two feet long, which can be

California sea-lion (*Zalophus californianus*)

inflated so that it stands almost erect. The bull is twenty feet long and nearly two tons in weight. The cows are much smaller. The **northern elephant seal** lives off the Pacific coasts of North America, feeding on vast quant- ities of squid. Once a year these seals congreg- ate to breed and it was at this time that hunters' rifles took a fearful toll of them in man's lust for valuable seal oil, until by 1870 they were almost exterminated. The few remaining were

Northern elephant seal (*Mirounga angustirostris*)

Pygmy pig (*Sus salvanius*)
Wedge-tailed green pigeon (*Sphenurus sphenurus*)

Collared pig (*Sus scrofa*)

on Guadalupe Island. These were given protection by law and now they are increasing in numbers and are overflowing onto neighbouring islands and onto the coast of California. Very occasionally stragglers have been seen as far north as Alaska.

THE MIDGET PORKER

The midget of the entire pig family, small as a cigarette package when he is born and standing only one foot high as an adult, bears the appropriate name of the **pygmy pig.** Moving about in groups of a dozen, this pig roams the deep forests and tall grasses on the foothills of the Himalaya Mountains north of India, digging into the ground for roots, worms and insects. For this, the seventeen-pound pygmy pig is equipped with a powerful, flexible snout, which ends in a tough, flat disc. With his remarkable nose, as useful to him as is the elephant's trunk, the grey-brown pygmy pig can push aside logs, overturn rocks and dig into the earth to get at anything edible which catches its notice. The pygmy pig may live to the ripe old age of twenty-five or thirty years. The unusually small size of this pig is brought out in a striking manner by comparison with

62

Moose (*Alces americana*)

the **wedge-tailed green pigeon,** which is also found in the same parts as the pygmy pig.

RETURN OF THE NATIVE

Through the dense underbrush of steaming forests in south-east Asia roams a big brown-grey wild pig with a distinctive band of white on its face and another around its neck. It is known as a **collared pig.** Its long, thin snout looks like that of a wild boar, and the sharp teeth curving out of its lower jaw resemble the two powerful tusks of any of the wild pigs. But the wrinkled-skin collared pig is a domestic pig that has gone wild again. (We speak of domesticated animals that have returned to the wild as "feral".) Usually quite placid, it spends its time trotting through the underbrush of its native Borneo, Sumatra and Java, and feeding, as all pigs do, mainly on vegetation, such as grass, leaves, roots or fallen fruits. Occasionally it will stop to roll in the mud to cool itself, and

to scrape annoying parasites off its skin. Like so many wild animals, including the wild pigs, the collared pig is not dangerous unless molested, and will only attack in panic or in self-defence.

BIGGEST WANDERER

The gigantic, cumbersome moose – whose European counterpart is known as an elk – is the largest of the world's numerous deer family. In the northern United States and Canada, three races of dark-brown **moose** roam the forests and marshlands. One of these races lives in the eastern parts of North America, from northern New England to the barren stretches of Labrador in Canada. Standing as much as 7½ feet at the shoulder and measuring nine feet in length, a bull moose may weigh three-quarters of a ton, and it carries the biggest antlers of any living deer, with a span of up to 78 inches. In summer the moose are solitary.

Okapi *(Okapia johnstoni)*

in autumn they pair for the breeding season. They browse on leaves and bark and often wade into lakes to nibble their favourite water lilies and to escape from the flies and mosquitoes. When the heavy winter snows restrict their food, moose come together in groups to trample a wide tract of snow into a hard-packed oasis, called a "yard". There the huge males, together with the hornless females and their babies, consume all the vegetation in the area. Then the group lumbers off to make a new yard. So they move about, feeding, until the spring thaw allows them to start wandering again through the well-watered forests.

64

dappled sunlight and deep shadows, it moves about in a family group, browsing leaves and young shoots. Its deep colouring makes it inconspicuous in this gloomy environment, its only protection against animal and human enemies alike.

BEWARE OF GIANT BULLS

A giant among bovines is the tremendously powerful **gaur,** chiefly found in north and central India. Just over six feet high at the shoulder, with head and horns upraised, the bull presents a magnificent and awe-inspiring front with his curving horns, nearly 3 feet long. A distinctive feature of the head is a conical cap between the horns, pointing forwards. The cows are slightly smaller and less impressive, although they also are agile and untiring in climbing the hilly slopes to feed on grasses and bamboo. Herds generally average about a dozen cows dominated by one big bull. He is shy by nature, and always ready to move away on scenting intruders. But when his rule is overthrown by a younger and stronger bull, he goes off to lead a solitary life. It is then that he becomes dangerous, as though soured by age and defeat. Instead of retreating, he becomes aggressive, and the sight of this four-footed Goliath in full head-on career has often been the last sight on earth for unwary hunters.

Kouprey (*Bos sauveli*)

Gaur (*Bibos gaurus*)

A ZOOLOGICAL ENIGMA

It is almost incredible that an animal as big as an **okapi** should have remained undiscovered for so long. As large as an ox and existing in quite large numbers, its presence had been rumoured for a few years before Sir Harry Johnston sent a piece of strikingly-marked skin to London in 1901. Even then it was thought to belong to some sort of forest-dwelling zebra. It was not until some years afterwards that some okapis were captured and transported to zoos. A distant cousin of the giraffe, the family resemblance is noticeable, although its neck and legs are not so long as those of the giraffe. Unlike its relative, who lives on the plains, the okapi lives in the depths of the forests in Equatorial Africa. Here, in the

THE CAMBODIAN MYSTERY

First heard of in 1937, the **kouprey** (koupray or couprey) is popularly known by the people of Cambodia as the Wild Ox of the Forest. A slow, rather clumsy beast with a certain keen fierceness, it has seldom been seen by a white hunter. It is not easy to penetrate the thick jungle growth during the rainy season, so the kouprey is most likely seen during the dry season which lasts from November to March. This is a very rare animal; not more than 1,000 are in existence. No yoke has ever adorned its neck, in fact, none has ever been held in domestic captivity. Its thirty-inch horns, with their pronounced curve, have near the tip what looks like a cuff of gossamer-like hairs. The kouprey is sixty-six inches high and over eight-feet long. Both sexes have a pronounced dewlap, and the strong tail is four feet in length, its tip like an unbraided buggy whip.

DOCILE GIANT

A huge creature measuring up to six feet at the shoulder, the **Indian water buffalo** is good-tempered, easily domesticated and a patient beast of burden. Although indigenous to India and the Far East, it readily adapts to many different climatic conditions. Now rare in a wild state, it lives in groups of twenty to fifty in humid forests always near water. An excellent swimmer, it is perhaps more agile in water than on land. It is not aggressive, and will attack only if it feels it is in danger. Having poor eyesight it has trouble seeing its enemies, yet once aroused it will fight with all the force of its incredible strength. A pair can pull three combined teams of trained draught oxen backwards in a tug-of-war. Even a tiger is no match for it. Yet a domesticated water buffalo will allow a child to lead it.

The docile nature of the Indian water buffalo

Indian water buffalo *(Bubalus bubalis)*

Indian water buffalo *(Bubalus bubalis)*

is in sharp contrast to the aggressive character of the African species, sometimes called the Cape buffalo although it ranges over the whole of Africa south of the Sahara. In fact, although the two are called buffaloes they are not very closely related. One of the first differences we notice between them is that the horns of the African buffalo meet across the forehead and have sharp ends that curve back. The horns are much more like meat-hooks and look as if they are meant to be used with savage intent. In addition, the African buffalo grows to a larger size. Both are about the same height at the shoulder but the African buffalo is slightly longer in the body and its weight may go up to 3000 pounds against 1800 for the water buffalo.

FLESH-EATING VEGETARIAN

The brighest-coloured coat among all African forest **duikers** belongs, without doubt, to the small, agile **zebra antelope,** which inhabits deep forests in Sierra Leone and Liberia. Its coat is brilliant orange and gold, banded with soft blue-black stripes, and it is a most attractive sight seen against the tangled bushes and vine-covered trees as it browses the tasty leaves. Like all forest duikers, the zebra antelope sleeps

nearly all day. Only at night does it leave its hiding-place to forage until the first rays of the morning sun send it bounding back to concealment in the dense undergrowth. But not all its food is vegetable. In fact, so great is its appetite for meat that when in a zoo the zebra antelope will eat chopped meat put into its cage, scorning vegetables, fruit and cereals placed with it. And duikers kept as pets have been seen to kill and eat birds, such as poultry.

Banded duiker or zebra antelope
(Cephalophus doriae)

THE TIMID DIVER

"Duiker" may seem to be an odd animal name, but it is really a most appropriate title for the graceful little antelopes that abound in bush country and deep forests in Africa. Duiker is a Dutch word meaning "diver", and plunging into the dense undergrowth at the first hint of danger is perhaps the most outstanding trait of the timid duikers. So shy are they that many Africans have never even glimpsed a duiker, despite the fact that there are many more of them concealed in the undergrowth than there are big game roaming the African plains. The largest of all forest duikers, that range from the size of a terrier upwards, is the donkey-sized **yellow-backed duiker** of the forests from Sierra Leone to Uganda. Standing three feet at the shoulder, the yellow-backed duiker has the brown coat characteristic of the many species of duikers, but the many shadings of its back glint with warm golden highlights in the rising tropical sun when at dawn it ends its night-long search for leaves and grasses – and also for fat snails and insects. Although duikers are

Yellow-backed duiker
(Cephalophus silvicultor)

supposed to be almost strict vegetarians there have been reports, from people that have kept tame duikers, of them killing and eating birds.

TRULY FOUR-FOOTED ANTELOPE

Antelopes are members of the same family as goats and oxen, although they look much more like deer because most of them are so slender and graceful. The **klipspringer,** like the majority of antelopes, lives among the rocky areas and cliff ravines over much of eastern and southern Africa. It has rather sturdy legs and a thick coat of stiff bristle-like hairs, the males only having tiny spike-like horns. Its tiny rounded hoofs give it the appearance of tripping about on tip toe. Above all, it is a terrific jumper, and more sure-footed than any goat. It can spring from the ground and, with all four feet placed

Klipspringer *(Oreotragus oreotragus)*

tightly together, land on a pinnacle no bigger than a silver dollar.

THE STONE-HEAD

The **gerenuk** gets the first part of its scientific name from the fact that its skull is as hard as a rock. Called the antelope giraffe because of its long slender legs and giraffe-like neck, its long ears and, in the males, the lyrate horns make its small head seem even smaller. The gerenuk is found on the dry African scrublands from Ethiopia to Kenya. Travelling in small groups it is very difficult to surprise because one of the group is always on the alert. Gerenuk are easily frightened and very cautious, and will visit water-holes and other grassy spots only after sundown. They are hunted mainly for food, but inexpensive leather goods are produced from their hides, the horns being too short for trophies. In the competition for food, the long legs and neck of the gerenuk give it a distinct advantage, enabling it to rise onto its hind-legs to reach up to foliage that is out-of-reach for many browsing animals. However useful this long neck may be when feeding, when skulking through the bushes it lowers it into line with its back.

Gerenuk (*Lithocranius walleri*)

Saiga antelope *(Saiga tatarica)*

DESERT ANTELOPE

Gusts of wind cause the sands to swirl and fly over the flatlands of Central Asia. Through sheets of sand, with head held down, a strange-looking antelope comes running. It is the **saiga,** undaunted by dust and wind storms. Its swollen moose-like nose, with nostrils overhanging the mouth, contains a hair-lined channel which filters the dust. The saiga is probably the most unusual-looking of the antelopes. With lyre-shaped horns that are ringed in front and about a foot in length, it is the size of a small sheep. Its summer coat is of thick hair, dull yellow in colour; its winter coat is almost white and sheep-like. Living on the plains of Central Asia, it was so reduced in numbers from being hunted that there was real danger of its becoming extinct. Now, completely protected, it is much more numerous.

LOOKS CAN BE DECEPTIVE

The ungainly **takin** ambles down from the Himalayan crags with its bloated nose sniffing the ground. It gives the appearance of desperately trying to keep the rock path in focus, and the dull expression in its eyes seems almost to suggest that it is failing to do so, but the surefooted way it negotiates the edge of the precipice leaves no further room for doubt. In its frequent migrations from the highest mountains of Burma, Tibet and China to the valleys below, in search of tender bamboo fodder, it makes good use of its singular and

adept mountaineering abilities. Despite its bulky and clumsy body, short massive horns and stocky legs, the takin is related to the fleet, mountain chamois. It looks more akin to a mountain sheep on which some prankster has stuck an ox-head. Its curly, woolly hair makes it look like a left-over from a pre-historic era. In contrast to its ungainly shape, it is a brilliant yellow. A Chinese species *(Budorcas bedfordi),* the

Takin *(Budorcas taxicolor)*

golden takin is rated as the most brightly-hued of all mammals. Its entire front coat is a shiny metallic gold.

KINDNESS PAYS

It is thanks to Vittorio Emanuele II that the **alpine wild goats** or **ibex** are still in existence. In 1821, in the Grand Paradise zone of Val d'Aosta, Italy, the hunting of these animals was forbidden. A still stronger decree was issued in 1850 to the effect that hunting within the domain of the Royal Reserve was absolutely prohibited. Today, there are over two thousand of these animals roaming the mountains of Switzerland, Italy and Austria. The alpine ibex can tolerate extremely cold weather; its diet consists of moss, lichens and tree bark. After the mating season it is solitary. Easily recognized by its hard, knotted, scimitar-like horns, its

Alpine wild goat or ibex *(Capra ibex)*

African elephant *(Loxodonta africana)*

most common enemies are man, and raptorial birds such as the eagle, which will carry off the young for food. Once hunted by man for food the alpine ibex is now hunted largely for its trophy, its head and horns. Butting is its only defence, but it is capable of killing a man with this.

HERE COMES THE REAL KING

In contrast with its more good-natured Indian relative, who for centuries has been domesticated for work in the Far East, the big-eared **African elephant** is aggressive and fierce-tempered. The Africans have never made any attempt to subjugate these mammoth creatures, the largest and most powerful animals living on land. The gigantic six-ton, eleven-foot high African elephant is instantly ready to charge if its wonderfully sensitive trunk scents the faintest danger on the grassy plains. With its immense ears alert and spread wide, and its six-foot long trunk raised high above its head, the elephant trumpets through the bush, rampaging like a cyclone, ready to gore an enemy with its ten-foot tusks, or to trample it underfoot. When undisturbed, the blackish-grey African elephant

roams in affectionate and highly disciplined family herds of about twenty to forty, over the plains of Africa, south of the great Sahara Desert. Through the hottest hours, the close-packed herd dozes under the trees. As the burning tropical sun sets, they wander away to their favourite watering-hole, to drink a daily ration of fifty gallons of water, and to frolic in the water's depths, with all the zest of a small boy paddling with his friends in a pond. The drinking and frolicking finished, the African elephant lumbers off into the forest for serious eating. And serious eating it is! Each day an elephant consumes about two-hundred and fifty pounds of leaves and branches, with a small sapling or two for dessert; and a herd feeding in the forest sounds like a tropical storm. Enormous branches are broken off with a sound like rifle shots. Whole trees come thundering down. But if the herd scents danger, these giants steal away in single file as silently as a summer breeze, without snapping a single twig. Intelligent and fierce, the gigantic African elephant has been largely spared subjugation by humans. The famous thirty-seven war elephants which the Carthaginian general Hannibal took over the Alps on his unsuccessful invasion of Italy in 219 B.C. were African. But Hannibal learned in a battle later, with the Roman general, Scipio Africanus, that the bad-natured African elephant was quick to panic, fly into a rage, and trample Hannibal's own soldiers. Only in the Congo, in recent years, have a small number of these aggressive elephants been broken in for pulling ploughs and hauling timber, and made docile enough to export to the world's zoos and circuses. Even this venture, begun by King Leopold of Belgium in 1900, has been a tedious and dangerous task, strewn with the bodies of native trainers who met their deaths on the two-hundred pound tusks or under the six-ton mass of their evil-tempered pupils.

1. **Emperor penguin** (*Aptenodytes forsteri*)
2. **King penguin** (*Aptenodytes patagonica*)
3. **Rockhopper penguin** (*Eudyptes crestatus*)
4. **Jackass penguin** (*Spheniscus demersus*)
5. **Adélie penguin** (*Pygoscelis adeliae*)
6. **Fairy penguin** (*Eudyptula minor*)

THE SWIMMING BIRDS

The **penguins** stand erect and dignified in a group on the frozen Antarctic beach. With their shiny white shirt-fronts, long black coats and stubby tails, they look like a lot of important old gentlemen dressed for dinner. It is easy to understand why explorers call them "little old men in evening dress". Penguins not only look like men, they act and move in a very human way. Unable to fly, they walk clumsily; indeed when in a hurry they often slide across the ice on their bellies, propelling themselves with their wings. But they are most at home in the water. Suddenly there is a commotion and the group becomes agitated. With all the skill of a swimming champion an **emperor penguin** dives into the water, streaking at twenty-five miles an hour, speedily and efficiently catching numerous small fish. Emperor and **king penguins** have a habit in common; they do not build nests, but brood their single egg on top of their feet, protecting it with a fold of skin in front. Others, like the **Adélie penguin,** dig a shallow depression in the ground which they line with stones, bones, moss, and grass. The **rockhopper penguin** has also been on an underwater food-finding expedition. When this is over it leaps out of the water like a salmon and lands on a rock several feet above the surface. It takes a short rest and two others waddle up to it, and after what looks like a confidential chat, the three flightless, swimming birds energetically set off on one of their enthusiastic climbing expeditions, clambering for hours over rocks and ice-floes, apparently simply to pass the time. The **jackass penguin** is not quite so carefree or sociable. It likes privacy and will sometimes bite intruding explorers. The jackass penguin's colony vibrates with a confusion of queer sounds resembling the braying of donkeys, the honking of horns, the snoring of old men, and the mooing of cows! Much gentler is the tiny **fairy penguin** of Australia. It averages only twelve to eighteen inches in length and is covered with a thick mat of feathers rather like a mixture of wool, fur, and down. Moisture does not penetrate its "waterproof" coat, and even after sixteen hours in the sea it can land with perfectly dry feathers.

All penguins live in the southern hemisphere. One species lives on the Galapagos islands, just south of the equator, but this is where a cold current flows up along the coast of South America.

Palm nut vulture (*Gypohierax angolensis*)

THE VEGETARIAN VULTURE

Half-way down the west coast of Africa, in the sunny land of Angola, where gnarled mangrove trees bear sweet fruit in salty tidal basins, a solitary white **palm nut vulture** is soaring. Although a true vulture it has nothing of the repulsive appearance of the better-known, carrion-eating species. Nor is it like them in habits, its main food being the nuts of the oil and raffia palms. Occasionally it is seen boring holes in the stems of the palms for insect grubs, and it sometimes takes crabs and other crustaceans from the mangrove swamps. It will sometimes feed on carrion, but this is usually in the form of fish stranded on the shore. Only very rarely does it take a small bird.

Hanging parakeet (*Loriculus aurantiifrons*)

THE JUNGLE MIDGETS

Among the smallest members of the parrot family are the sparrow-sized **hanging parakeets,** of south-east Asia. The name "lovebird" was given to an entirely different kind of parakeet, from Australia, but it could with equal justification have been given to the hanging parakeets. A pair of them will sit for hours, beak to beak, and while doing so seem lost in rapture. These green birds, with a splash of orange, seem determined to enjoy each other's company to the full. They roost hanging upside-down, in the manner of bats, suspended in clusters from the slender branches of trees. The female of a near relative, in Ceylon, builds a nest of the edges taken from green leaves, which she carries to the nesting-site tucked under her rump feathers.

RADAR-EQUIPPED BIRD

The **oilbird,** or **guacharo,** of northern South America is one of the strangest living birds. It spends practically the whole of its life in darkness, nesting and roosting deep in caves where no light penetrates. Like the bat, it uses a kind of "sonar", making audible clicks and picking up the echoes from these to find its way about in these caves packed with huge colonies of oilbirds and their incredibly fat nestlings. The twenty-one-inch long oilbird is related to the whip-poor-wills and nightjars, but is the only vegetarian in this otherwise entirely insect-eating order of birds. It eats the fruit chiefly of the oil palm. At nightfall the oilbirds leave the cave to feed, sometimes travelling more than fifty miles to find ripe fruit, which they pluck from the trees while hovering, with wings whirring. They return to the twittering underground colony before sunrise.

LEISURELY INSECT-CATCHER

Among the strangest of all birds is a little, owlish, mottled creature with a yawning, frog-like mouth, that flies only at night in the woodlands of far-off Australia. While all the other birds in the forest are scurrying around to catch insects, the **tawny frogmouth** dozes lengthwise on a branch in the warm sunshine. When night comes, it flutters lazily off its perch and onto a branch or stump to watch for insects, such as beetles and caterpillars. It also takes centipedes, and occasionally a mouse. The remarkable feature of this bird is that although it has the wide boat-like bill of the nightjars, suitable for

Oilbird or guacharo (*Steatornis caripensis*)　　　　**Tawny frogmouth** (*Podargus strigoides*)

snatching up insects in flight, it picks its food off the ground, and does so in a leisurely manner. It has, however, the superb camouflage of the nightjars, and if disturbed by day it stretches obliquely upwards, so that it looks like a broken stub of a branch.

Frogmouths belong to a different family from the nightjar, although the two are related. Their food is anything that crawls, such as caterpillars, beetles, centipedes and scorpions.

Hoopoe (*Upupa epops*)

INSANITARY BEAUTY

The **hoopoe** is so-named for its call, a musical *Hoo-hoo-hoo* that carries a long distance. It spends its winters in India and Africa, migrating north into Asia and Europe for the summer. Its reddish-brown plumage, with the wings and tail barred black and white, is crowned by an erectile crest of feathers tipped black-and-white. It feeds on insects, using its long, down-curving bill to probe the earth in search of them. By contrast with the beauty of its plumage, the nesting habits of the hoopoe are filthy in the extreme. Most nesting birds are particular about sanitation, the parents removing the droppings of the nestlings. Not so the hoopoe. Added to this mother and young secrete a foul, glandular smell not unlike that of the skunk.

The hoopoe has attracted attention from the earliest times. It is pictured on tombs and temples in Ancient Egypt, and the god Horus, who represented the sun, was depicted with a hoopoe's head on his staff. In the Middle Ages the hoopoe was connected with magic and the occult, and its flesh was supposed to have great healing power. Certain parts of its body were supposed to improve the eyesight and restore failing memory. But the Jews, in Old Testament times, were forbidden to eat it, largely no doubt because of its insanitary habits.

Fire-breasted Indian flower pecker
(Dicaeum ignipectus)

A MEAL OF MISTLETOE

In the Himalayan mountain forests, as high up as 11,000 feet, dwells the brilliantly coloured **Indian flower pecker.** With its fiery breast bright in the sunshine it scours the very crowns of the trees, picking insects out of the flowers. Its diet also includes nectar and anything else that is sweet or sticky, its curved beak being especially useful for poking about for mistletoe seeds. The mistletoe is a treetop parasite and rightly or wrongly the three-inch fire-breast is blamed for spreading its seeds throughout the slopes. It flits about the mountainous country solitary or in pairs. The flower pecker's nest is shaped like a pear and to find the entrance you must seek out a slit at the top. The inside is lined with soft materials such as spider's webs, silk from cocoons and down from fluffy seeds.

THE BLUE HONEY CREEPER

The small dull-coloured bird flies rapidly from branch to ground and back again, carrying small twigs, moss and grass to finish her neat cup-shaped nest. While she builds the home, her mate, the brilliantly coloured deep sapphire and turquoise **blue honey creeper,** preens his feathers and feeds. Perched on a branch, he pokes his long, slender curved beak deep inside a flower where his sensitive tongue sucks up the sweet nectar and any small insect sheltering inside. His bright plumage and vivid red legs make this bird a superb spectacle, as he flutters and swoops through the air. He does absolutely nothing to help his mate. She lays the eggs, incubates them, and feeds her chicks alone.

But when the chicks are grown and ready to fly away, the male blue honey creeper gradually loses all his gay colouring and becomes like the female, a dull green, until the following spring.

FRIENDLY MOUNTAIN TRAPEZE ARTIST

High in the Swiss Alps, where all is stillness amid the snow-capped beauty of the mountains, the playful "khi, khio, khio" of a bird breaks the silence and goes echoing through the crystal-clear air. It is the lively chatter of an ebony-black **alpine chough,** wheeling and diving among the precipices where it makes its nest on stony ledges. Climbing high, and then diving on closed wings, the glossy fifteen-inch bird somersaults away the spring and summer days in its Alpine home, while other Alpine choughs, who live as far east as China, trapeze gaily near their own lofty mountain nests. The Alpine chough lives at such high altitudes, that it has even been seen frolicking at dizzying heights on 29,000 foot Mount Everest, the highest mountain in the world. Wherever this yellow-beaked relative of the crow makes its home, the valley-dwellers know when winter is approaching, for then flocks of these friendly birds come down from their mountain nests, to pass the winter in warmer regions below. While begging for bits of food in the valley villages, the amiable Alpine chough is some-

Blue honey creeper
(Cyanerpes cyaneus)

Alpine chough (*Pyrrhocorax graculus*)

in its native haunts in the Amazon basin, in South America.

A SHOCKING FISH

On a sunny afternoon in 1941, two Brazilian fish-research workers were walking across a plank over a pool filled with **electric eels.** The plank tipped, the men fell in and were instantly killed by 400–volt shocks from the eight-foot snake-like fish slithering in the waters' depths. The electric eel is the most powerful and dangerous of the thirty-five or forty known electric fish, and has been known to have knocked out a horse twenty feet away. In its shallow fresh waters of Brazil, Colombia and Peru, this fish must come up to breathe air every fifteen minutes, or else drown, a rare feature amongst fish. It has gills, but these are little used, respiration being through patches in the mouth richly supplied with blood-vessels that take oxygen directly from the air. The electric eel's shock equipment occupies the rear four-fifths of the body. It is used for defence and for seeking out and stunning small fish which form its food.

THE GORGEOUS OFFAL-EATER

One of the most beautiful fishes of the South Pacific is really nothing more than a gorgeous scavenger. This glamorous-looking creature is called the **sea bat,** but no bat ever had the glor-

times captured and put into a cage, where it makes an affectionate pet, often living to sixteen or seventeen years of age.

MEET THE BIG FISH

The biggest freshwater fish in the world and yet one of the most graceful is the **arapaima** of South America. Its huge body has been known to grow as long as fifteen feet and weigh four hundred pounds. But its average size is generally about seven or eight feet long. Although its Christmas-coloured body (green scales tapering into a red tail) is so massive, it is one of the most graceful fishes when in motion, gliding smoothly through the water. This tropical colossus is an easy fish to remember by its shape. Unlike most fishes its head is more tapering than its tail end, the latter being blunt and adorned with three fins. It is these the fish uses to hollow out a nest in the sandy lake beds

Arapaima (*Arapaima gigas*)

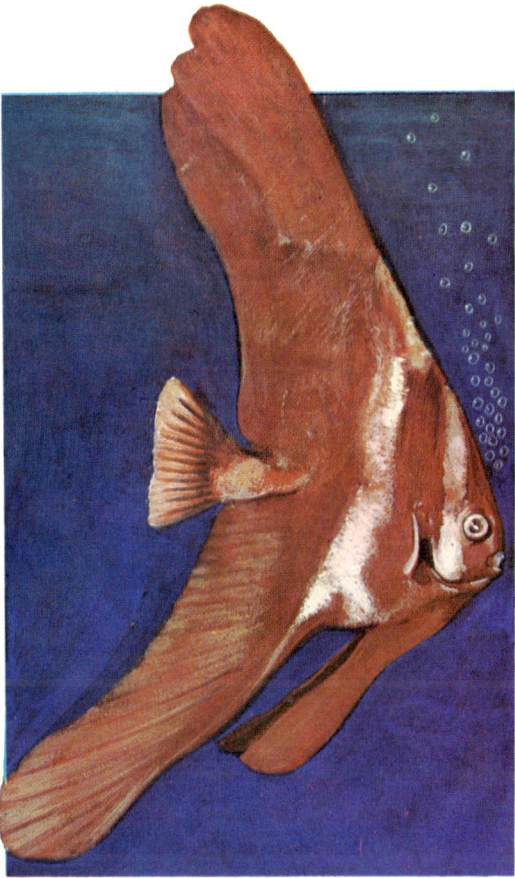

Sea bat *(Platax orbicularis)*

← **Electric eel** *(Electrophorus electricus)*

Moreover, the lateral line of sense-organs takes a decided curve just behind the head to impart almost a hunchbacked appearance. The turbot, and a few other flatfishes, is exceptional in that it comes to lie on the right side, whereas most flatfishes are lying on the left. The Romans used to keep turbot in their fish-ponds, for culinary purposes, and the fish has always been especially favoured as food. One item of its own diet is small herrings feeding on the sea-bed.

THE HIPPO OF THE FISHES

The **halibut** may reach a weight of seven hundred pounds, a length of ten feet and the age of forty years. Its Latin name happens to be

Turbot
(Scophthalmus maximus)

ious colouring of this charming, tangerine-orange fish. Its two-foot body is higher than it is long and its fins are wing-like, which is its only resemblance to its namesake. Its particular taste in food is probably due to its being completely toothless, but it also eats small plankton animals as well. In captivity it has proved to be an excellent pet: amusing, likeable and very beautiful to watch, not to mention being an economical pet to feed.

THE HIDEOUS DELICACY

The **turbot**, like others which are known as flatfishes, begins life as a "normal" fish, with an eye on each side of its head. As the young turbot increases in size, one eye migrates through the skull to take up a position on the other side of the head. The fish itself also comes to lie on one side. The total result is that all flatfishes are eventually lying on one side permanently, with two eyes on one side of the head, a somewhat distorted skull and a rather twisted mouth. The distortions are especially pronounced in the turbot, giving it a somewhat hideous face.

Hippoglossus hippoglossus, and it could well be called the hippo among flatfishes. On the European side of the North Atlantic ocean it is found as far south as the Bay of Biscay; on the American side, as far south as New York. This colossus, the biggest of the flatfishes, is

Halibut
(Hippoglossus hippoglossus)

Dwarf salamander (*Manculus quadridigitatus*)

soft knob of a sticky tongue which can be shot out for a considerable distance. The tongue is like a mushroom, free all round, but attached to the lower part of the mouth by a stalk. It has great elasticity as it stretches out and then returns to its former position between the jaws filled with numerous small teeth. Not only has this salamander an unusual tongue, and differs from the amphibians in not swimming, it is also unusual in the salamander family in having only four toes on each limb, whereas others have five toes on the hind feet.

A SOUTH AMERICAN KING

In the luxurious growth of the foothills of the Cordillera in South-West Colombia lives a South American king of all toads, **Blomberg's toad.** True to type, this nine-inch-long giant loves a moist climate and thrives on an insect

one of those that come to lie on its left side, with both its eyes on its right side. Another oddity about this giant is its breeding habits. Unlike most fish, it usually spawns in winter, rather than spring, each female laying as many as 2,700,000 eggs in one season.

UNIQUE OF ITS KIND

The **dwarf salamander,** at its longest, is only three inches in length and the greater part of that is tail. A slender, graceful little creature it is found among rocks in the swamps of Carolina, Florida and Texas, and nowhere else. Although an amphibian, it does not swim but spends its life on land. There it searches, or lies in wait, for insects which it catches with the

Blomberg s toad (*Bufo blombergi*)

Crested iguana (*Conolophus subcristatus*)
Marine iguana (*Amblyrhynchus cristatus*)

diet, so has settled in an area with a rainfall of 150 inches. Here it lives, changing its skin once every three to ten days and, after kicking its arms and legs free, it rolls the old skin into a ball and swallows it. Not only is its size spectacular, but its handsome coloured skin, although

Great grey marsupial tree frog
(Gastrotheca ovifera)

poisonous, excites admiration, so it is hardly surprising that each of the world's zoos wants a specimen for display. Many, however, are still waiting, for this distinguished Colombian is a newcomer to collectors; it was only discovered as recently as 1951.

A WORLD OF THEIR OWN

Two species of dragon-like iguanas live on the Galapagos Islands together with the giant tortoises. They are found nowhere else. The **crested iguana** lives on the land and is strikingly coloured. Up to three and a half feet long it feeds on vegetation, including a spiny cactus, and it has long been a matter for surprise that the lizard swallows these long spines, which pass through it undigested. The second species, the **marine iguana,** is four and a half feet long, and it feeds on seaweeds at low-tide. Coloured blackish-brown, it spends much of its time on the black lava rocks. Occasionally two males, with heads down, will quarrel over territory, but first they try acts of intimidation. Perhaps the most remarkable feature of the marine iguana is that although it can swim and dive well it seldom swims far, and if thrown into the sea immediately turns and makes for the shore.

UNZIP A FROGLET

The Cloud Forest of Rancho Grande in Venezuela, where the clouds continually drift in from the plains and the trees are loaded with mosses, orchids and ferns, is the home of the **great grey marsupial tree frog.** This frog has curious little round "suction pads" on its toes for tree climbing. Torrential rains sluice away or sink into the mossy jungle floor, and there

is no still water. The mother frog therefore carries her eggs – and there may be twenty of them – in a pouch low down on her back. When the female is laying her eggs she raises herself on her hind legs so that the eggs roll down the inclined plane formed by her back, and through a slit-like opening into the pouch, the male assisting this by pushing with his feet. The eggs are heavy with yolk, and when the young leave the pouch they are not tadpoles, but are already fully formed little frogs. Within ten seconds after hatching they are agile enough to jump over the mother's back, and when eight hours old will try to capture the big moths on which the adults feed.

For a long time after the marsupial frog was first discovered by scientists there was considerable speculation about how the eggs found their way into the pouch. Then somebody managed to film a pair of these frogs mating, and it could be seen that the male was helping. Then came the puzzle, about how the froglets were able to leave the pouch. Only recently was it learned that the female holds it open with a hind toe when they are ready to leave.

Cuban anole *(Anolis equestris)*

THE CUBAN KNIGHT

There are 165 species of anole lizard in tropical America and the largest is the **Cuban anole** a foot and a half long, of which two-thirds is tail. This is not a great size, compared with other lizards of this region, but the Cuban anole more than makes up for its small size by its war-like appearance. Clad in an armour coat of small scales from the tip of its tail to its head, it deserves its other name – the Knight Anole. But, unlike the mediaeval knight who, once unhorsed, was incapable of any movement, this lizard is incredibly agile. Like all anoles it has expanded toes and fingers, each with an adhesive pad on the underside, which enable it to run up smooth, vertical surfaces that would halt

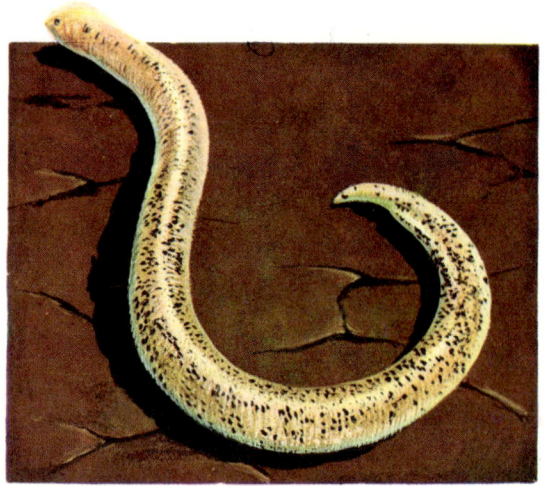

Arabian worm lizard (*Diplometopon zarudnyi*)

Cylindrical or eyed skink (*Chalcides chalcides*)

most other creatures. Although the anole is sometimes found in gardens its home is in the forests where, using its strong hind legs, it leaps among the branches in search of insect food.

ALMOST LEGLESS LIZARD

The family of lizards known as the skinks contains more species than any other family of lizards. Skinks are found over almost all the land masses of the world, and in the islands of South-east Asia, as well as in the forests of Asia, they are more abundant than any other lizards. Yet we hear little about them, and even where they are abundant they are seldom seen. Some of them live underground, but most of them live on the surface, remaining hidden in the leaf-litter, under rotten logs or under large

stones. To a large degree they keep out of sight because they have developed long slender bodies, and their legs have, at the same time, become weak. Some skinks have lost their legs altogether. The **cylindrical skink** of Southern Europe, also known as the **eyed skink,** could be said to be almost on the point of losing its legs altogether.

A REPTILE PUZZLE

Throughout the scheme of animal classification there are small groups whose exact place in that scheme is uncertain. One of these is a family which, for want of a better term, have been called **worm lizards.** These are found more especially in Africa, but there are some in southern Asia and also America. They have the long cylindrical bodies we associate with earthworms. Their bodies are covered with a soft skin, and as in earthworms it is marked with rings. In addition the worm lizards spend their lives under the surface of the ground. They

Elephant beetle (*Megasoma acteon*)

feed mainly on ants and termites, and the females lay their eggs in the nests of these insects, to be incubated. Although in some respects they are reptilian, they lack legs, are able to move forwards and backwards, and they progress by vertical undulations of the body, not by sideways wriggling as in snakes and legless lizards. So, for want of better knowledge of them, they are grouped in a separate family among the lizards.

THE TUSKED TERROR

An elephant lumbers into view carrying a long trunk, flanked by two ferocious-looking tusks. But this "elephant" is only two inches long and is really a beetle. Rising from its head are three horns, a long one in the centre and two shorter ones on the sides, and it is these that are responsible for its name – **elephant beetle.** They seem to be of little use except perhaps to make it look fierce or for use occasionally in fights with other males, but most of the time their size probably cuts down the insect's speed and ease of movement. The females are without them. There are several species of this curious, dark-coloured beetle, one of the largest being found in North America. Since the larvae eat roots and the adults eat foliage and flowers the elephant beetles are something of a pest.

CHEMICAL DEFENCE

Slowly, on a remote and lonely battlefield, the large attacker, a toad or a bird, closes in on the tiny **bombardier beetle.** Confident in its greater size the larger creature has underestimated the beetle's ability to look after itself. The beetle carefully assesses the range and leaves its decisive defensive manoeuvre until the very last moment. Suddenly the bombardier

Bombardier beetle (*Brachinus crepitans*)

Click beetle *(Pyrophorus noctiluca)*

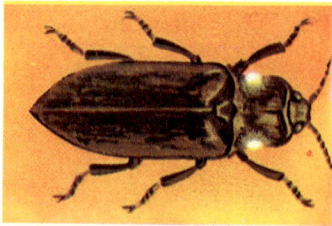

HEADLIGHTS IN THE DARK

To a small, tropical American insect, this **click beetle** must look like the equivalent of a flying bubble-car, with its two yellow head-lamps and one red rear light glowing in the dark. Four click beetles together give enough light to read by and once, during the building of the Panama Canal, a doctor had to use their light to perform an operation. The local peoples still use the beetles, tied to wrists and ankles, to light their way in the dark. If one of these beetles falls on its back, it bends its hinged body until it can hook its sharp spine into a notch on its abdomen. When this is released, it produces the famous "click", and at the same time the beetle shoots up into the air, usually landing right side up. The click beetle larvae are, however, pests. They are usually called wireworms and cause considerable damage to crops by their attacks on the roots.

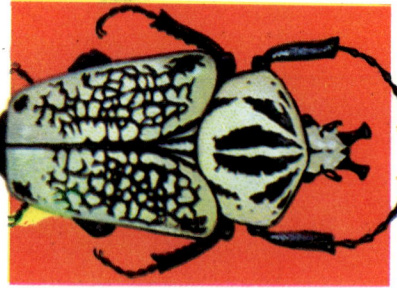

Goliath beetle *(Goliathus giganteus)*

beetle turns its back on the attacker and fires a salvo of "shots" from its rear end. With a "pop" each shot explodes and releases a cloud of pungent poison gas, which has a highly detrimental effect on the attacker. With its enemy helpless the bombardier beetle makes good its escape, unscathed and none the worse for the encounter.

THE GENTLE GIANT

Even though the **goliath** is a giant among beetles of the Scarab family, it is much affected by the weather. On fine days this five-inch insect flies out to gather a meal of pollen from the flowers but in bad weather it remains sheltering under loose bark and debris. The beetle's thorax is patterned with black lines on white. The wing-covers are brown. The whole insect is covered with a velvety pile which can be rubbed off. Children in tropical Africa where the beetle lives sometimes catch it and make it fly in circles on the end of a string, its black wings beating powerfully in an attempt to get away. From eggs laid in rotten tree stumps or moist ground hatch white worm-like larvae without legs. These feed on vegetation, burrowing into the ground for roots. Finally they pupate and later comes the change into adult beetles which fly away to decorate the forests with their presence.

THE BIRD-SIZED MOTH

Fluttering through the South American forests is an insect much larger than many birds. Although the **owlet moth** has a wing-span of one foot and is the biggest moth in the world it is seldom seen, for it only flies by night. The pair of compound eyes helps the male hardly at all in locating the female in the dark, so he must use his extraordinary sense of smell. Strong and fast in flight, the wings of the owlet moth help it to cover long distances on migration. At each fresh stop its well-developed tongue goes to work for feeding upon nectar, ripe fruits and other such sweet substances. The caterpillar of the owlet moth feeds on the leaves of plants both living and dead. Before it can reach the adult stage it must pupate. It burrows into the earth and constructs a simple cell where it can spin itself a cocoon. In due course there breaks through this covering an insect larger than many bats.

THREE STRANGE SPECIES

Since the days of Solomon, ants have been credited with the ability to plant and harvest crops for their food. The **seed-eater ant,** to which Solomon refers in the Bible, does collect and store seeds in its nest underground. Sometimes these are moistened by rain seeping into the nest and germinate. The sprouting seeds are then carried by the ants to the surface where, discarded, they may root and grow – giving the

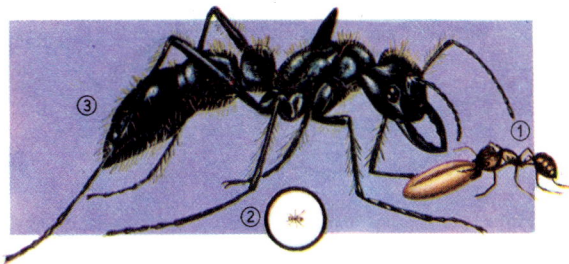

1. **Seed-eater ant** (*Messor barbatus*)
2. **Pharaoh's ant** (*Monomorium pharaonis*)
3. **South American giant ant** (*Dinoponera grandis*)

appearance of planted gardens around the ant nest. Equally well known but much more commonly seen is the tiny **pharaoh's ant** which is a household pest in nearly every country in the world, moving in continuous caravans along the floorboards and under sinks in our kitchens, bedrooms and living-rooms. This tiny creature became world-wide through being a stowaway on ships, even on those crossing the oceans, and it can be seen in first class cabins as well as crowded tourist bunks in nearly every ocean steamer. Unlike its tiny relative, the **South American giant ant** is a stay-at-home. One of the most primitive ants in the world, it dwells in the Amazon basin in South America. This is the largest ant we know – nearly two inches long – and very fierce. As it runs over the ground it looks like a mechanical toy – moving first one limb and then the other – as if weighed down by its heavy armour. It is older than Solomon, more ancient than the Pharaohs of Egypt, and may outlive mankind himself.

Owlet moth
(*Thysania agrippina*)

Slave-maker ants *(Polyergus rufescens)*

Freshwater planarian *(Dugesia tigrina)*

UNDERGROUND BONDAGE

In our history books we read that slavery was finally abolished throughout most of the world a century ago. But in the animal kingdom, the practice of keeping slaves is still very much alive, especially among the war-like, needle-jawed **slave-maker ants** of Europe and Asia. These fierce insects procure slaves by first sending scouts out of their teeming nest, to find the burrow of less powerful ants. As soon as the prey is discovered, the slave-maker ants swarm as a vast army in a direct route to the victims, slaughter the workers, and carry the larvae back to their home. When the prisoner larvae have hatched, the young ants start a life of servitude for the slave-maker ants. One of their duties is to feed their masters, whose sharp, sickle-shaped jaws would seem to be terrible weapons for piercing enemies' heads, but are

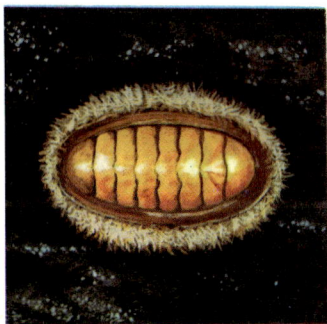

Chiton *(Rhyssoplax discolor)*

totally useless for feeding. In fact, so helpless is the fierce slave-maker ant in feeding itself, that without its slaves it starves to death, even though surrounded by masses of food.

A TEN-HEADED WORM

This curious animal is a small flatworm or **planarian,** living in freshwater in the United States, but there are species like it throughout the world. It bears two eyes, but one thing missing from its face is the mouth, which, unexpectedly, is situated in the middle of its body on the underside. A planarian eats flesh, dead or alive, by thrusting out a long pharynx or feeding tube from its mouth, breaking up its prey by a sucking movement and swallowing the fragments. Perhaps its most peculiar feature is its ability to reproduce by breaking up, each piece growing into a new flatworm. If you cut a planarian into pieces each piece will grow into a new worm, complete with head, mouth and eyes. It is possible, by splitting a worm down the middle and preventing the wound from healing, to produce an animal with two heads side by side on the same body. This can be repeated until eventually a ten-headed monster is produced.

ARMOURED CAR?

The **chiton** is the most primitive member of the mollusc family, identifiable by its eight over-lapping armour-plates, which are linked by a strong muscular girdle, the margin around them being ornamented with small spikes. It has no tentacles, and no eyes. It avoids the light by holding tight to the surfaces of rocks, in shallow seas or between tide-marks on the shore, by its muscular foot. The mouth is underneath, at the front of the body, and gills are located in a groove running back on either side from the

Giant cattle leech *(Dinobdella ferox)*

mouth. The chiton uses its file-like tongue, known as a radula, beset with numerous horny teeth, to tear up and swallow small algae growing on the rocks. If dislodged from its rocky foothold, the chiton will partially roll up, but because of its homing instinct, about which little is known, it can later make its way back to the spot where it was found.

FEROCIOUS BLOODSUCKER

Since the days of the early civilizations of China and North Africa leeches have been used in medicine; and "blood-letting" has been regarded as a cure for almost every kind of illness until a very few centuries ago. Even today leeches are sometimes used for curing the sick. The ringed body shows that a leech is related to an earthworm, but only distantly. It lives in water or on moist earth and moves by means of a strong sucker at each end of the body, but it may release its hold and swim with undulations of the body. It feeds by gripping the skin of its

1. **Trigger fish** (*Balistes carolinensis*)
2. **Sea-urchin** (*Diadema setosum*)
3. **Sea-cucumber** (*Holothuria impatiens*)

victim with its front sucker, making an incision with its jaws and sucking up the blood that flows from the wound. Leeches are most

numerous in tropical countries, and an animal going to drink, or to bathe, may leave the water with numerous leeches on it, which have been attracted to it in the short while it was in the water. Most leeches are small and suck only small quantities of blood, and if there is any truth in "blood-letting" being good for a person, we could say they do little harm and might even do good. That, however, cannot be said of the giant leeches of south-east Asia, which are up to a foot long. What people think about them is reflected in the scientific name, for "Dino" means "terrible" and "ferox" means "ferocious". The soldier crossing a river in Malaya seems to agree with this description of the **giant cattle leech** in the foreground.

CUT-AND-THRUST AROUND THE REEF

It is often said that hardly has a new weapon been invented than somebody invents some form of defence against it. The same could be said for the animal kingdom, and whenever we find an animal with a good means of defence we also find another animal that can penetrate its defence. The **sea-urchin** shown here has long spines which should be enough to deter any aggressor. Not only are they long and sharp, and capable of inflicting a poisonous wound, but the urchin can direct them at an intruder. Nevertheless, the **trigger fish** has a sort of beak-like mouth armed with closely-set teeth, which enable it to break open mollusc shells and to reduce the spines of the sea-urchin, as well as the limy box in which it lives, to fragments. The trigger fish then eats the flesh of the sea-urchin. The **sea-cucumber**, known as *Holothuria impatiens*, found in tropical seas, is able to shoot out from its rear end, when disturbed, long bluish-white threads. These are sticky and become wrapped around an intruder, making it difficult for it to move.

Luminous centipede
(*Geophilus electricus*)

Amphibious apple snail *(Gastropoda* sp.*)*

Another sea-cucumber lives in temperate seas, but it lives in holes and crannies in the rocks. To feed, this sea-cucumber pushes out the circlet of tentacles surrounding its mouth. These tentacles are slimy and trap tiny animals swimming in the water. The sea-cucumber then withdraws each tentacle in turn and curves it over to the mouth to be licked, just as a child licks one jammy finger after another. But this sea-cucumber sometimes has to leave its stronghold in the rocks to feed, and then it is in danger of being snapped up by a fish, against which it has no defence, once it is in the open.

UNDERGROUND LIGHTS

Centipedes are not insects, although closely related to them. Their bodies are elongated and made up of rings, each ring being armoured with a horny substance, known as chitin, the same material that coats the bodies of insects. Almost all the rings on the body bear a pair of legs, but the total number of legs is seldom a hundred, as the name implies. In temperate regions centipedes are small and keep well out of sight, in the ground or under logs, where they feed on insects and worms. In tropical countries they may grow to large sizes, up to a foot long, and these larger centipedes feed on mice, birds or frogs. In some parts of the world people eat them, or use them roasted and powdered as a medicine, which is surprising in view of the appearance and habits of centipedes. Several species of centipedes are luminescent, which means they give out a light. But a **luminous centipede** presents a puzzle. To begin with it is blind, so the animal is not lighting its own path. Moreover, it lives more or less underground, and we only see its light when it comes to the surface. It does not use its light for attracting the opposite sex, when breeding. And since the centipede lights when we touch it or drop it into water, or when attacked by ants, we can only suppose that in some way it is protective. How we do not know, but it may be that the light dazzles the attackers.

1. **African giant snail** *(Achatina fulica)*
2. **Slug** *(Limax* sp.*)*

3. **Door shell** *(Clausilia tridens)*
4. **Philippine snail** *(Helicostyla festiva)*

AN EXCEPTIONAL SNAIL

The **amphibious apple snail,** living in the marshes of Central and tropical South America, has a breathing cavity divided into two parts. One contains a gill, the other is a lung. By thrusting its long breathing tube to the surface of the water, the snail can take air into its lung. It can then close this half and open the other, so that the gill comes into action. All the time, the lung-breathing and the gill-breathing alternate regularly, with the result that whether the snail is on land or completely submerged in water, it is able to breathe.

A COLLECTION OF GARDEN PESTS

Here are three of the several thousand different kinds of **snails,** together with one common species of garden **slug.** All these crawl about on land, chewing vegetation, and in many places being pests to farmers and gardeners. What is the difference between a land snail and a slug? A snail is a long, soft-bodied creature that carries a protective shell or "home" with it wherever it goes. When danger threatens, or when food and moisture are scarce, it can withdraw into its little fortress and remain until conditions are favourable for it to venture out. Some snails have been known to stay in a deep sleep inside their shells for four years, without taking any food or water! A snail usually has two pairs of tentacles on its head, one pair having a sense of touch, the other bearing eyes. A slug unlike a snail, has either no shell, or, at best, a thin shell-like plate embedded in its body. It also has two pairs of tentacles. At the far left in the picture is the beautiful *Helicostyla festiva*, a native of the Philippine Islands. Its coiled red shell is covered with a thick membrane, which becomes transparent when it is wet, disclosing the ruddy tints of the shell underneath. The huge brown snail, second from the left, is the **African giant snail,** truly a giant among snails, measuring nine inches long and weighing a full pound. The damage which this snail has done to plant life in the eastern half of the world is almost staggering. In 1847, the African giant snail was taken by a shell collector to India, and with its eighty thousand teeth it has eaten its way across the face of Asia, leaving devastation in its wake. Now in the South Pacific Islands, where it was introduced as a possible article of food, the African giant snail is wreaking more destruction than all the bombardments of World War Two. The orange-hued creature at the top right is the only slug in this collection.

It is a common garden slug, which like most slugs, avoids bright sunlight, and crawls about at night feeding on plants. Like all its relatives, it glides on a trail of slime secreted from its foot. This mucus is so thick, that it would protect the slug even on a razor's edge. When the slug finishes feasting on a plant, it returns to earth the easy way. It simply crawls to the end of the nearest leaf or twig, and slowly lowers itself to the ground on a thin thread of its own secretion. At the bottom right of the picture is the land snail named *Clausilia tridens*. It is one of many species that carry a thin plate, known as an operculum, which seals the entrance to the shell. When *Clausilia tridens* retreats into its shell the operculum snaps shut like a little lid, keeping the snail safe and snug inside the shell.

Common cuttlefish
(*Sepia officinalis*)

JET-PROPELLED INK-POT

The flat piece of hard white material wedged between the wires of a canary's cage is the internal shell of the **common cuttlefish** which feeds many other animals besides cage-birds. Living in European waters it moves through the green depths of shallow waters, its two large black eyes searching for shrimps, squirting water to disturb the sand in which the shrimps are hiding. It seizes them with two long arms, which are in addition to eight shorter arms covered with suckers. The cuttlefish swims at a high speed by jet-propulsion, a technique it used long before man invented it, which drives

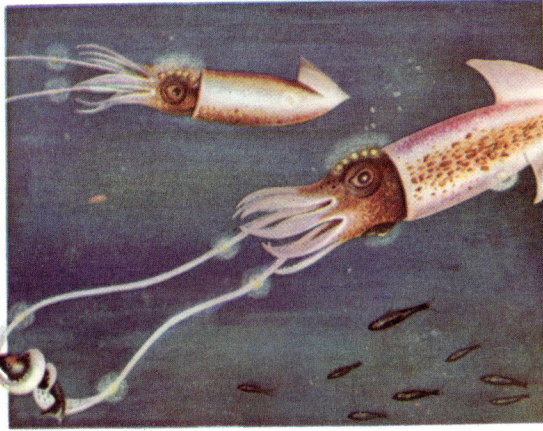

Deep-sea luminous squid (*Thaumatolampus diadema*)

distance. It seizes its prey with two of its ten arms, which are longer than the rest and carry suckers at their tips. A horny parrot-like beak is used to tear the prey apart. This invertebrate is an avid eater that blushes at the mere sight of food, by expanding the pigment cells over its body. The deep-sea luminous squid is an excellent swimmer, and careers backward through the water by spurting jets from a funnel beneath its head, using its tentacles for steering. To escape enemies, this squid, like all squids and octopuses, throws out a fluid, then turns pale so that it is invisible and slithers away, leaving its bewildered pursuer swimming in this cloud. But the smoke-screen thrown out by this deep-sea squid is luminous, not black as ink.

its six to ten inch body through the water. Enemies that pursue it are apt to be baffled when the cuttlefish lets out a cloud of black ink, or sepia, which forms a kind of smoke-screen. This sepia was used by the ladies of Ancient Rome as a cosmetic. Later, it was made into ink and sepia paint.

SQUID WITH A SMOKE-SCREEN

A mile down in the ocean deeps total darkness reigns, broken only by occasional flashes of light from the bodies of light-producing deep-sea animals. One such creature is the **deep-sea luminous squid,** whose two bulging eyes are ringed with luminescent organs to lure inquisitive crustaceans and small fish within striking

MOLLUSC WITH A BABY CARRIAGE

The ancient Greeks who sailed vast oceans to conquer distant lands, called the eight-inch **argonaut** "the sailor", because they believed this mollusc sailed in its shell, raising its arms to the prevailing winds. In the twentieth century an English zoologist, T. H. Huxley, corrected this idea, pointing out that only the female argonaut has a shell, which she uses not as a boat, but as a baby carriage. The mother

Argonaut (*Argonauta argo*)

Argonaut (*Argonauta argo*)

argonaut carries her eggs about safely in her frail, ridged, outer covering, and jet-propels herself through tropical and semi-tropical seas by shooting jets of water from a tube under her head. She can even swim completely out of her shell to seek the small fish which form her food. This versatile sea-dweller can also change colour, from brilliant blue to pale rose, simply by expanding or contracting the tiny pigment cells in her skin. The argonaut is also called the

Paper Nautilus, because her spiral shell is as thin as a sheet of stationery.

A MOUTHFUL OF FIRE

This animal is found on the coral reefs of the Bahamas and West Indies, swimming around by means of little paddles along the length of its body, feeding on small, soft-bodied invertebrates, tearing them apart by spreading wide its stout jaws and tugging in the prey with its powerful throat muscles. The **fire worm** has, perhaps, the best defence of any of the sea-dwelling worms, known as the Polychaetes, many of which build protective tube-homes for themselves. No fish will eat this animal, for it has earned its name. The soft-looking, fur-like, white tufts along its pink sides are in fact stiff bristles which pierce the mouth and stomach of an unwary predator, causing pain like the touch of a red-hot needle, and enabling this eight-inch-long juicy meal to paddle around quite fearlessly under the eyes of shoals of hungry fishes.

Fire worm (*Hermodice carunculata*)

THE WALKING WORM

This velvet worm-like animal from Panama lives in damp places, sheltering during the day under logs or stones and promenading on its twenty-four pairs of legs only after it has rained, or at night, in search of prey. **Peripatus** eats a variety of insects and worms including those it finds already dead in rotting leaves and damp crevices. Near its mouth is a pair of glands from which it can spit a rubber-like solution, used in self-defence and perhaps to subdue insect prey. Should this solution get onto its own velvety, wrinkled back, Peripatus sheds its outer skin, and with it the blob of hardened slime. The babies are half-an-inch long when they are born, exact replicas of their parents, that wander off on their own, at a few weeks of age. There are numerous species of Peripatus, in South Africa and Australia as well, all unlike any other animal, except one whose imprint is in limestone rocks laid down 600 million years ago. Neither worm nor insect, Peripatus is a link between the two.

Peripatus (*Macroperipatus geayi*)

A REFUGEE FROM THE SEA

The class of animals known as the Arthropoda, or jointed-legged animals, includes the insects, crustaceans and spiders, as well as some smaller groups such as millipedes and centipedes. By far the most numerous are the insects, and these are found almost entirely on land or in the freshwaters. Only a half-dozen or so species live in the sea. The next most numerous are the crustaceans, and most of these live in the sea except for land crabs and woodlice, which live on land, and a relatively few species that live in freshwater. Among the more familiar crustaceans living in the sea are the shrimps and prawns found in shallow waters. These are often found swimming in the tidal pools left on the shore when the tide is out. Prawns may, therefore, be described as typically marine. There are, however, a few species of prawns which, while almost indistinguishable, except to the eye of an expert, from the truly marine prawns, live in brackish waters or even in freshwater. One of them, shown in our picture, is found especially in Southern Europe, in the estuaries and in rivers. It shelters among the eel grass and seaweeds, its semi-transparent body making it almost invisible in the water. It is, in fact, a

Freshwater prawn (*Palaemonetes vulgaris*)

marine crustacean that has left its native habitat, the sea, and has sought refuge in rivers.

To most people shrimps and prawns look much alike except for size, so we are apt to call the small ones shrimps and the large ones prawns. Furthermore, as we go from one English-speaking part of the world to another the names have been used so indiscriminately that there is the utmost confusion. The name "shrimp" comes from an ancient Nordic word that means small or shrivelled. The name "prawn" does not appear until the Middle Ages. True prawns

Giant sea spider (*Colossendeis proboscidea*)

have a saw-toothed "beak" between the eyes, which is hidden in our picture.

DEEP-SEA COLOSSUS!

Sea spiders belong to a different class from land spiders, to which they are only distantly related. Most of those found in coastal waters are little more than an inch across. In the ocean depths, however, their size seems to increase with the depth. The largest known is the **giant sea spider,** with a span of twenty-four inches or more, living at ten to twelve thousand feet below the surface. As often happens with deep-sea animals, this one is found not only in the great depths of tropical oceans but also in the shallower icy waters of the polar seas. Sea spiders are nearly all legs and no body. They feed on small forms of marine life. When first hatched a sea spider has only three pairs of legs, but another pair grows after the first moult, giving four pairs; and some may grow five, or even six pairs of legs. Some of the sea spiders living in shallow seas often find odd refuges, under sea cucumbers or in the umbrellas of jellyfish.

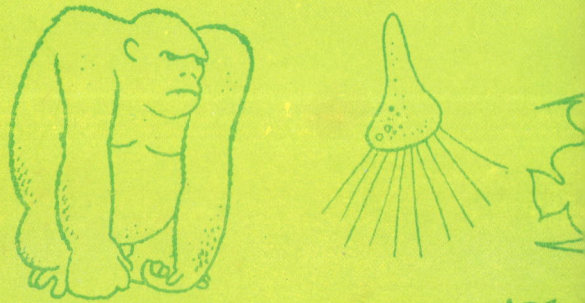